A TASTE FOR HAPPINESS

MICHEL DAVID-WEILL
PATRICIA BOYER DE LATOUR

A TASTE FOR HAPPINESS

Copyright © 2014 Michel David-Weill and Patricia Boyer de Latour
All rights reserved.

ISBN: 1500565164
ISBN 13: 9781500565169
Library of Congress Control Number: 2014912876
CreateSpace Independent Publishing Platform
North Charleston, South Carolina

Introduction

I have lived my life in joy. I have had the good fortune to live in several places around the world, to get to know many interesting cities, which has required a certain amount of organization on my part to avoid spreading myself too thinly and to retain a modicum of detachment in order to be happy. I have been careful to do just that. It is not so easy; it requires a bit of tenacity. My professional, family and private responsibilities have helped me a great deal in this respect, but strangely enough, at the age of twelve, I was already the person I was to be forever. Maintaining a state of happiness in the long term while always keeping in mind what is truly important is a good way of looking at life. So many people end up losing themselves to such an extent that they become nothing more than the perception of what other people have of their lives... I would not go so far as to say that I was conscious of having a particular destiny, but very early on, I sensed that I could reconcile everything that was important to me and I shaped myself in such a way as to resist external influences.

I do not set myself as an example, but I feel I am a link between the past and the future.

I have divided my time living between the United States and France, which is not that common a thing to do. At present – and this will no longer be true thirty years from now when countries like China, India or Brazil will have a great deal more influence –, my perspective has been greatly expanded by this fact. All my life, I have had ideas that were rather unusual, and it is not necessarily a bad thing to try to allow people to hear them. Deep down, it amuses me to write down what I think, even though some might find it shocking. There is true joy in being a free man.

I do not feel any particular need to justify anything at all and, as someone who lives in the present, I have no desire to recount the details of my existence. But I am quite certain that no one in future will live the life I have lived. I am one of the last representatives of a lost world, a world that my grandfather knew before me. The Lazard Company no longer belongs to me, my art collections will one day be broken up and scattered. Nothing lasts forever. And yet, I am not nostalgic, quite the contrary; it is the present that interests me more than anything.

The world is beautiful; we can live every moment intensely. This is the path that I have walked, in the hope of taking with me anyone who wished to join in my adventure, but without being pretentious enough to draw any conclusions. I have therefore desired to bear witness, without affectation but with accuracy, to what I love, what I have seen, felt, come to experience and understand.

Happiness in Spite of Everything

I have a taste for happiness. In my opinion, the ability to be happy has nothing to do with external circumstances… It is something you are born with. Happiness is a gift, and it has far more to do with temperament than with objective facts. It is also a choice, just as long as you are in good health and not burdened with true problems of survival. But we have all known people who had everything they needed to be happy and yet were not. And others who, despite going through terrible ordeals, succeeded, through a form of unique grace, to transform their lives into a celebration. I believe that any day when you have not been happy, even for a fleeting moment, is a day lost. There were times at Lazard when I was plagued with worries, and now that I am no longer concerned with them, I find myself dreaming of that surge of passion that runs through you just as you are making a decision, that rush of adrenaline, like a drug that my body became used to, a rush that I no longer feel... But the freedom of finding myself in a pleasing environment, as is the case today, surrounded by charming people, having time to look forward to life, the ability to make the most of the moment, to read, to sleep better, all these things are truly magical. I would be very ill-advised not to be satisfied with all this, and I am actually very conscious of my good fortune. And so I savor these pleasures without thinking I have a right to them, yet appreciating my extraordinary privilege to freely enjoy them every day. In addition, my new activities within Eurazéo, a public company specializing in buying companies through *leverage buy-out* in which I hold the post of President to the Board of Directors, the field of art in which I am both privately involved and act on behalf of museums, my private affairs, which I realize I have terribly neglected up until now, and the charity work I am involved in, I find all these things interesting... I am really not blasé. One of my daughters recently said to me: "What's good about you is that there are so many things that give you pleasure!"

This taste for happiness is a foundation that is stronger than anything, and I believe that it is not that common. Most people do not actually loathe unhappiness... Unhappiness reassures them, perhaps because it is familiar, and thus relatively comfortable. Certain people even think that by revealing their unhappiness they might attract attention and gain compassion from others. From the time I was a child, I discovered, perhaps out of egotism, that I found unhappiness deeply tedious. As soon as I am unhappy, I am bored. Consequently, I try to disengage myself as quickly as possible from such emotions, because they holds nothing satisfying for me.

There is a virtue in being happy: you can help others more with a certain type of joy. If you are happy, many problems dissipate; there is a light through the fog, it makes life easier in all its forms, both within the family or at work. Even though I do not believe in a positive afterlife, I am no less happy. I am a joyful pessimist who is often surrounded by serious, sad optimists!

At a very early age, I was certain that all one needed to succeed was the desire to do so. Without the illusion of believing that whatever one does is of the least importance, I was convinced that, whatever I did, I could only succeed. It is essential to do something, even if it is of little interest, but it must be done well! On the other hand, one of my fundamental beliefs is that it is preferable to commit to a specific path. People often think that what is essential is the life they choose. I am not of that opinion. A chance series of events determine your existence: place of birth, family, education, the people you meet, etc. You find yourself in business or in politics, you run a farm, you become a banker or give guided tours of a castle… without having much say in the matter. But, from that point on, each of us should freely commit to something. If you put some effort into it, you will survive. If there is no meaning to anything, why not act? Most people say: if there is no meaning to anything, let's do nothing. I don't see the logic in that… If there is no meaning to anything, let us act, because life is better when we put some effort into it, and it is also rather more entertaining. Besides, I think that even if you continually succeed, you can only fail in the end. Every career ends badly.

Early on, I could feel my solitude, a solitude without anguish, but a reality nonetheless: I was alone and I knew it. The experience of living through a war as I did as a child was undoubtedly a determining factor. I knew what it was like to live in hiding. I changed my name; I could have no friends, none that were long-term, in any case. I was isolated, far from the privileged social background in which I had been coddled since my birth in Paris in 1932, and I had to be careful of what I said... In June 1940, my mother, my sister Éliane, who was two years my junior, and I all left for Spain. At the time, my father was still in the army. My paternal grandmother and grandfather, and my aunt Antoinette, their youngest daughter, came with us.

Crossing the Spanish border affected me greatly. We had the impression that we were watching a country collapse... It was a horrifying defeat that each person passionately felt and I still remember it as if I had been personally wounded. Then, when my father was finally released from the army, we went back to France to join him. André Meyer, his business partner, had left for the United States in May 1940, so he had to go to discuss the bleak future of the Lazard Bank he lead with the existing authorities in Vichy, in particular with the Commissioner for Jewish Affairs responsible for the Aryanization of French businesses.

Lazard's offices had moved to Lyon, so we lived there during the winter of 1940, before leaving for Cannes where I went to school by bicycle, on the streets that leads up to Cannet. And I was in the fifth year there twice! I hadn't done the third or fourth year because I didn't go to school in the winter of 1939 or the winter of 1940. So I skipped two years. After that, I skipped another two, the fifth and sixth years. My school career was a little strange.

HAPPINESS IN SPITE OF EVERYTHING

My father left for New York by himself in 1942, a few months before the United States declared war, and we had no word from him until the end of the hostilities. We were supposed to go and join him there, but my mother wanted to wait until her son Jean, whom she adored, had the opportunity to come and say goodbye to her in Cannes from Paris; Cannes was still in the unoccupied part of the country. He was arrested in the autumn of 1942 while trying to cross the Spanish border to join the Free France forces. We waited for his return in vain. He died of typhus at the end of the war, after having spent years in the Dora concentration camp where the V1 and V2s were built. My mother never got over it...

My memory of Jean, my older brother who was twenty years old, is that of a young god in a Greek arena. He was a very open, kind, handsome, active boy, gifted at astronomy and mathematics. He had attended Centrale (an Engineering School), he was a pilot, loved motorcycles and diving and was the most excellent skier; and he was extremely kind to me. I felt that he was very different from me. I was clumsy, I didn't even know how to run, and he excelled at everything. He didn't seem to experience any of the difficulties that I encountered. But I hardly know anything about him... I was seven; he was thirteen years older than me, which is a lot at that age. Such was my impression.

When my mother finally decided to go, we were unable to obtain the permit needed to leave France in time. No one wanted to deal with it. I even have in my possession a copy of a letter handwritten by my mother to M. de Brinon, Minister of Foreign Affairs in Vichy, who was shot in 1947, asking him to intervene, which he absolutely would not do. Before the war, he was Director of *Information*, a newspaper that belonged to the Lazard Bank, and had been a friend of my parents.

And so we lived in Cannes until the spring of 1943; that was when my maternal grandmother learned she was on the list of people to be deported. She was Belgian, and therefore a foreigner, so she was in danger once the Germans entered the Free Zone, as at that time, the Germans decreed that foreign Jews should be deported. She lived with us and regularly played cards with the woman who owned the Hôtel Montfleuri, which was occupied by the Gestapo; she saw my grandmother's name on the list and had telephoned to warn her. So, we left... It was then that we changed our identity. According to my false papers, I had been born in Amiens and was named Wattel. I have forgotten many things that happened then, but, in retrospect, and even if it is somewhat surprising, everything about my life at that time seemed normal to me, and still does to this day. It is everything that happened to me since that seems less normal.

If nothing else, this experience taught me that what my contemporaries yearn for - a stable, permanent, organized and predictable world - is a complete illusion. I have never believed in it, in any way whatsoever. When the World Trade Center collapsed on September 11, 2001, everyone believed we were entering a new world. Personally, I felt as if I were going home. I have always had the impression that you could make the majority of your own luck by putting in the effort and by being rather self-confident; but not all your luck, because everything can be swept away by chance, for no real reason, and also because you can never be absolutely certain about anything.

Instead of being crushed by this idea, it gave me added joy, because if everything is always possible, then the best might also happen. As a child, I could never imagine that peace would return. Even though I had read history books and understood on an intellectual level that peace always follows war, I didn't believe it. War was normal; but peace, I had no idea what that meant; it was inconceivable to me. And to a certain extent, it has remained so.

When we fled from Cannes, we were taken in at the château de Montrosier near Rodez, in the Aveyron region, by Mme de Billy. She had told my mother to come and stay if there was any hint of trouble. Her father collected châteaux. And that is how we came to rent Béduer, which used to be owned by her father, in the Lot region.

This isolated property jutted out over the countryside; we remained there from September 1943 until March 1945, openly, for all to see. We were hidden in broad daylight. When a car drove up, we didn't know if we would find the Gestapo or the Resistance. Some of the Béduer farmers asked me one day, "Where is your father?" I didn't know what to say, so I improvised, "He's dead." When I got home, I asked my mother if that had been a good idea. "Yes," she replied, very good." It might seem a bit odd, but the atmosphere in which we lived was relatively normal, even though we could have all been taken by the Germans at any moment. There was my maternal grandmother, my sister, and many of our employees who were very loyal and had stayed with us; there was a cook who had known me since I was a baby, a butler and a chamber maid, who were married and had also been there when I was born, and my governess...

One day, a friend of my mother's who wished to help her, Mme Margot Noblemaire, whose husband was Director of the *Wagons Lits*, came and told her that she knew of a network that managed to get Jewish children into Switzerland. My mother asked me what I thought of the idea. I didn't want to go: I fear the unknown more than the known; I would have the same opinion today. You may think that finding a safe place is the best idea, but there are serious risks in trying to secretly cross a border…

Why take such a risk when we were more or less settled in and things were going rather well? We were living on top of a volcano, but I knew the volcano. France is relatively large; we were in an isolated spot in the countryside, even if the Germans did pass through from time to time. And, to a child like me, in a certain way, it was an adventure. And I still have a taste for adventure; I enjoy the feeling of breaking away from normal life. Any time there's a clash somewhere, I'm on my way! When I was a student at *Sciences Po*, one of my favorite pastimes was going on demonstrations. My political opinions were, however, already totally moderate; and this fact contributed to setting me apart during my student days, when everyone felt so passionate. There were Gaullists, Liberals, Royalists, etc. But since the only people who demonstrated were either from the extreme Right or the Communists, I used to alternate going to each of their demonstrations! Thank heavens, I didn't get myself noticed as a spy for either side, and I can remember seeing Le Pen, very present at the demonstrations of the extreme Right that I went to, and the Communists, one of whom rather touchingly said, "The Party is like a mother to me." Useless to point out that I didn't believe in either the New Order or the promise of that brighter future, but I enjoy the electrifying joy of the atmosphere of a fight: it makes you feel so alive. Perhaps I felt sufficiently on the margin of all the fisticuffs to be able to enjoy it with a kind of detached cheerfulness, as it had nothing to do with me. Yet I recall having attended the first great Gaullist meeting in Paris in 1948 and finding it appalling. I had the same feeling in May '68 when I tried to take part in a Gaullist march from the Place de la Concorde to the Arc de Triumph. I couldn't manage it and ended up following the demonstration by walking alongside it on the sidewalk. French Nationalism also has a slight whiff of Fascism about it which makes me feel uncomfortable. God knows that General de Gaulle could not be accused of being a Fascist, but there is a certain atmosphere about Gaullism that I find unbearable and which, in a crowd, becomes obvious.

The solitude in which I lived as a child went along with a certain amount of timidity rather well. That said, I have never met anyone who wasn't shy deep down. Shyness is the one thing in the world that we all have in common. But when it is combined with a certain sense of solitude, imposed by external events, it brings with it the habit of keeping enough distance from others so they are not in a position to cause you any trouble. All this brings about a desire to maintain one's independence, even if this means sacrificing what is natural in relationships with others. One of the virtues in this attitude, and there are many vices as well, is that you learn how to think independently: because it is unnecessary to compromise, which is the basis of all social interaction, you acquire the instinct of trying to think about everything that happens by yourself, and you are not satisfied until you have succeeded in forming your own opinion. I remember that in 1941-1942, when my father was still living with us in Cannes, my parents entertained some guests. Even back then, I was astounded by the stupidity and banality of the comments some of them made. I heard very competent people, people who were considered very intelligent and distinguished, saying things like, "the English cannot win" or "the English will win the war", without any valid reason whatsoever and a displaying a staggering lack of understanding.

Since I didn't go to school often during those years, I spent my time in a corner of the garden reading everything I could find in the library: Dante, Stendhal, Flaubert, Balzac, Maupassant... and even a book on economics by Charles Gide. I found all of it thrilling!

My mother was also very keen on literature and encouraged me – she had the time, partly because of the war – to immerse myself in Racine, La Fontaine and Colette, whom she adored. Strangely enough, I never read children's books, and never Jules Verne, for example, until much later, during the school holidays in Sous le Vent, in the Midi. I was delighted to discover the *Thousand and One Nights* in the translation by Delarue-Mardrus. "In the courtyard within a magical garden, precious jewels and candied fruit hung from the trees…", the very candied fruit brought from the French Rivera by Spanish

Jews who had fled the Inquisition, and which I adored. I also remember the *Tour du monde*, from 1860 to 1869 published by Hachette and written by a group of journalists who recounted their travels, a visit to Mauritius or an expedition to study the Incas' civilization... I have to this day, in Sous le Vent, all the books that belonged to my brother Jean, his books on Astronomy, for example; I still find their presence very moving. And close by is the complete hardback collection by San Antonio that my daughters gave me as a gift! I also kept the little books that the GI's had in their pockets when they disembarked in Provence in 1944 and which they left there... They mean a lot to me. Deep down, I realize that I was never a child. I don't even know what it means; I believe it's some invention by the English in the 19th century! To me, childhood was something adults invented, with no basis in reality.

I sensed I was different, and I accepted it. It was a rather mysterious feeling, because it is not mainly because of external reasons that one feels different, even if they do count: the war, obviously, the fact that I didn't go to school and having to use a different name... Feeling different, as M. de La Palice would put it, is realizing that you're not the same. And, as a consequence, finding that the people around you are not like you. For as long as I can remember, I have not found people to be like me. I am not totally integrated, not within a normal Catholic middle class, nor within a normal Jewish middle class, not within a vaguely left-wing intellectual group, nor within a conservative group, nor within the United States when I am there... To be absolutely honest, I will also say that coming from a wealthy family also makes you different, because the more you are defined from without, the less you feel part of something. People usually say, "You do not have the same problems as us" or "You can't understand, because you've never been in some situation or other", and so they contribute, not in marginalizing you, but in making you feel... different.

Moreover, being like other people provides a framework. Because I was different, I became attached to tradition, our family's tradition in particular, which has been handed down from father to son for four generations. When I was fourteen, I knew that I would become an investment banker, like my father and my grandfather, and I always felt an obligation towards the Lazard business, founded by the Lazard and Weill families in 1848 in New Orleans. Within this tradition, pride is combined with the modesty of providing a service, through which one might be in a position to deal with a country's fundamental issues, as was the case at Lazard's, when it was one of the two banks to have participated in propping up the Poincaré French Franc in 1924. At Lazard, there has always been the desire to participate in *relevant* acts, as the English say. I have always considered this word as one of the guides in my profession. It means that the act must be meaningful and carry a certain weight. Finding oneself at the heart of what is important is the essence of a company like Lazard and its *raison d'être*. Lazard plays the eminently respectable role of being a valuable advisor to business, which is the fruit of discussions between a group of people whose profession it is to find and define the best strategies in order to help improve business life.

I have always thought that given a choice between two courses of action, one of which earned twice as much money as the other, it was nevertheless better to choose the one that was *relevant*, even if it did earn half as much. Demonstrating integrity is also essential, showing that you deal honestly. Ideally and traditionally, the aristocracy values honor and the middle classes the concept of integrity; this obviously does not mean that other people are lacking such qualities, but it is rather normal that the middle classes, who define themselves by their material possessions, have been so concerned with honesty that they have adopted it as their basic moral criteria, because it must be said that temptation is far greater to someone in the middle classes than to someone who has nothing... A true member of the middle classes considers rules and regulations as superfluous, since anyone whose honesty is in doubt is excluded. And the fact that a man betrays their values even though he comes from the middle classes, would not prevent everyone from mistrusting him. "Never lose sight of the ethical issues": these were the last words my grandfather spoke on his death bed. Many people never adapt to the world of business, because they do not pay enough attention to this issue. My father, half jokingly, always used to say these wonderful words: "Beware of *self-made men*, because they believe it's their fault!" What he was implying was that, instead of realizing that luck, opportunity, and daily hard work allowed them to succeed; they have an unpleasant tendency to believe they are exceptional. And some of them are inclined to behave in ways that elevate their own interests to the status of virtues and necessities. They give themselves permission to anything they like in their desire for money, which can lead them to the most appalling excesses. The worst is when they cite their families to justify their activities. When that happens, you can be sure they are up to some mischief!

In truth, I have accomplished many things in my life to conform to tradition, family tradition in particular, but with no illusions, that is to say, without believing that it was the *only* solution, but thinking that it was a solution that suited me, a solution that made me happy.

Like my father and my grandfather before me, I never had links with a particular group, party or politician. Like them, I have a true respect for the State. In democratic countries, it is a mistake to think that the State does not count and that, consequently, as a business man, one has the right to take control of organizing the world of finance, which in reality goes beyond the rights of the individual. In a case that caused quite a stir in the United States a few years ago, a very brilliant gentleman managed, through "junk-bonds", to breathe life once more into companies whose economic growth remained, nevertheless, insufficient to entice investors; he thus imposed his own law, which he had absolutely no right to do, right until the moment when he ended up in prison. One must never forget that the State is sovereign and that it can sweep you away with the back of its hand.

Like my father and my grandfather, it was obvious to me that I had to try to work for others or for institutions that worked for the good of everyone. I was therefore delighted to hold the post of President of the Conseil artistique de la Réunion des musées nationaux (Advisory Art Council for National Museums), as they had before me. Like them, I am a member of the *Académie des beaux-arts*, which is a great pleasure, for the combination of a certain sense of grandeur with a certain amount of modesty makes this institution extremely valuable; here, one finds an equal mixture of eminent professors, craftsmen and artists, all of whom share a concern for taking action in order to encourage excellence in every sphere of artistic life.

Like my father and my grandfather, I know the United States very well, and it gives me great joy to spend part of my time there. My father lived in New York for many years and my grandfather was born in San Francisco. It was in the middle of the 19th century that the first waves of immigration from eastern France to the United States took place, and some of my ancestors, who came from that area, then left to cross the Atlantic. There was a Jewish family from Metz, the Arons, recorded in the census in the middle of the 18th century. This family played an important role in the French Jewish community, because their descendants included Raymond Aron and Jean-Paul Aron, the Noras (Arons spelled backwards), Maurice Rheims, Professor Jean Bernard, and the Wertheimer family. One of the Aron girls married a Lazard and another daughter married a Weill. So their children were first cousins. The first Lazards left for New Orleans in 1848, where they set up a business which, very typically, exported cotton and imported cotton fabric. And then, at the same time as the Gold Rush, between 1849-1850, there was a great fire in the city and a part of the population left for California. There, my ancestors continued to carry out the same profession, but in wool. They bought it from Basque shepherds and exported it, then imported the finished woollen products.

A TASTE FOR HAPPINESS

My great grandfather Alexandre Weill, full of enthusiasm, arrived in San Francisco at a very young age, at the same time as another of his cousins of the same age, Simon Lazard. It was due to their influence that the Lazards became bankers. The situation there encouraged it, for there were differences in the price of gold between California, New York and Europe. There was a kind of arbitrage in the price of gold from place to place, so they profited from these variations. In addition, they loaned money to various businessmen and industrialists. They did not like to speculate much and decided from the outset not to get involved with the gold mines. And that is how they became bankers. Then my great grandfather left California. In the meantime, all the Lazards returned to France. My great grandfather went to New York in 1880, and someone asked him a question, which I have never forgotten: "Why are you going to New York? It's much too late." By the time he went back to France, five years later, he had set up Lazard in New York. In the meantime, Lazard's London branch had been created, during the 1870 war, without any members of the family. The Anglo-Saxon world is therefore quite familiar to me, and it interests me a great deal. And yet, it would never cross my mind to change my nationality. I love the United States, but, like my forefathers, by tradition and to my great delight, I am, and always will be, French.

Art

No one in the world probably has better homes than I do. I only live in marvellous places and there are quite a few of them. Each in its own way is the perfect place to live: Paris, the Cap d'Antibes, Long Island New York, New York itself, London... And, in a certain way, these houses are each somewhat an expression of myself. Do they mean a great deal to me? No more than they reasonably should. For a long time I have believed that I could do without almost everything, and I still believe that today. Yet if I remain attached to my aesthetic environment, as I was to the Lazard Bank, it is because, in both cases, I contributed in helping a human enterprise endure – even though it too will disappear someday – for everything is destined to disappear...

For as long as I can remember, I have lived in a world bathed in the light of beauty. My paternal grandfather was a rather secretive, modest and imperious person who spoke passionately when it came to art. He lit up when he was near his collection, and today I feel much closer to him, to his taste and to his way of life. He was reluctant to speak, played the piano beautifully when he was alone, but stopped as soon as I came in. I was the only one of his grandchildren to bear his name and he loved me a great deal. I loved him as well and I would go over to him whenever he was smoking a cigar, because even then, I thought it smelled so good! I had the pleasure of living with him for a while after the war and the thing I found most appealing in him was his sensitivity. I remember his joy when standing in front of a painting by Watteau, or Fragonard or Corot... To him, the very breath of life itself was passed on through art, it was emotional, I could feel it. And it was moving, because he was old. At least, he seemed old to me at the time... He was the person whom I admired the most. Senior Partner of Lazard, he was also a great patron of the arts with encyclopaedic knowledge and, in the museum world, he was considered the moral authority *par excellence* and *the* person whose opinion was sought. When he was in his twenties, he donated the first Chinese statue to the Musée Guimet. He owned an exceptional collection of French silver, the likes of which have existed in only three or four places in the world, important collections of ancient Chinese bronzes and works of art from the steppes of the Louristan and Ordos and a very beautiful collection of painting from the eighteenth, then the nineteenth century.

The house he had built in Neuilly in 1900, on the Rue de Chézy, was delightful and not very different in feeling from the Hôtel Camondo. Every single object was beautiful – the furniture, rugs, paintings – and there were some fabulous drawings that one discovered by chance in some boxes. It was extraordinarily entertaining to visit his house. I would go up into the library, open a drawer and find engravings by Manet, Toulouse-Lautrec... In the back of a wardrobe was a collection of antique fabrics; in another, a collection of wine-tasting cups; in another spot, a collection of French snuffboxes... an endless series of unexpected and astonishing discoveries. It was like entering another world where the quality of his eclecticism became more apparent with each visit. There is nothing left of this house. It was destroyed; there is a building now where it once stood, and my grandfather's collections were stolen by the Nazis during the Occupation, then partially recovered, sold, scattered.

Not wishing to be in competition with his own father, my father, first furnished his Parisian apartment with works of art from the 1930s by Lurçat, Lipchitz, Giacometti, Masson, which were stolen from him as well, while he was in the United States... It was only while he was in New York, during the war, that he began to collect eighteenth century French paintings and furniture. Later on, he bought a marvellous house on Fifth Avenue. That was the first time since I was a very young child in Paris that I lived in an exceptional place. It was the reflection of a visually perfect universe, a world of extraordinary beauty and harmony. There was not a single object that wasn't French; it was all exquisite, including the view overlooking Central Park. We were at the same height as what is called the Reservoir, a rather large body of water in the middle of the park. Today the house no longer exists.

My father inspired within me the art of living, that is to say, a respect for beauty – you don't loll about on a Louis XVI settee – but also the tradition of recognizing beauty and using it to prevent it from becoming something sanctified. There were no display cases in my father's house, and there are none in mine either. These objects may be two or three hundred years old, but they are part of life and are in no way fossilized or out of reach, which happens far too often. He taught me something very valuable, but essential, and basically, something quite rare: how to live with beautiful objects in a normal way. He was a man for whom living amid perfection was natural. Neither luxury nor beauty were embellishments, ornaments or visible signs of wealth, but rather part of nature, like water or air. I am very conscious of this immense privilege, without a doubt the most important my father left me. I retained this lesson so well, which really wasn't a lesson at all, so well that he used to tease me by saying, "Judging from how you're starting out, you'll soon be living in Versailles, but you'll add another wing to it!" And he taught me all this simply by including me in his life; it was as natural as breathing. When he was interested in a subject, he was very serious-minded and wanted to know everything about it. When he was building a country house near Paris, he buried himself in books about architecture to decide how wide and high the balconies and windows should be in relation to the depths of the rooms. To plan the garden at the same house, he studied to find out which plants would grow the best there. And when he spoke about a business matter, he knew its entire history and all the figures. Since he was interested in French furniture, he became more than knowledgeable in the field, the way a respected professional would. I often accompanied him joyfully on visits to antique dealers and, rather amusingly, they were the ones who often asked for his opinion. When my father died, I had the feeling that an entire body of knowledge was lost with him.

ART

Today, Lazard's destiny is changing and my artistic universe has the transitory advantage of still existing, but it will disappear with me. My children will perhaps recreate another such universe in the same spirit, but it will not be the same. Since I have always been exasperated by individuals who placed things above people and who ruined their lives to own a particular place, I find it absurd to go too far in this direction. However, as long as these places exist and are the source of a certain aesthetic quality that exceeds the occupant who I am, that truth pleases me, as does the idea that there are, throughout the world, other aesthetically elegant places that are unknown to me. The reason why I love Stendhal's *La Chartreuse de Parme* so much is because he creates a beautiful world and never conjures up a sense of nostalgia over time that passes or that slight bitterness that comes with the awareness that everything is doomed, as does Lampedusa does in his *Le Guépard*... Stendhal provides delight. One is in that enchanted place ... one is there, so much so that one does not imagine for an instant that this world might ever disappear.)

This is exactly what I love about painting, because to paint is to be present, to seize a moment, to reconstruct it and recreate a world that will live forever, at least, for as long as the works of art last, because they too disappear or degenerate. I have the good fortune of owning a study for the *Fête à Saint-Cloud*, by Fragonard, in my opinion more moving than the painting of this subject in the Bank of France. It emits a presence that remains untarnished by any type of melancholy. It is often said that the landscape was almost invented by the Impressionists. But here there is already a landscape of impressions: a dramatic light illuminates the left side beneath the tent; it is evening; a tree has fallen out of its container; there is someone selling dolls... We have all experienced such moments of poetry in our lives. They are revived the moment we look at this painting.

If I were to attempt to sum up my taste in art, I would speak of jubilation, which is joy in motion, and a sense of grace where time is suspended, as in awe in the presence of God; or, to put it another way, eroticism and meditation. In any case, to be a work of art, it must strike a certain chord of joy within me. It might be physical, and then it is jubilation; if it strikes a moral chord, it is grace. Such an idea is inclusive but it also excludes many things. Any praise of ugliness, of ambiguity, of excess, of overindulgence, any derisiveness of beauty is foreign to me. Rather than Crucifixions, I prefer Annunciations, those moments of bliss when we are presented with pure femininity and hope. Today, the Christ of Colmar is praised to the skies – there is a flayed Christ, very painful – in the middle of this horrific scene; though very beautiful, it is in no way enchanting. I turn away and gladly sacrifice this type of art in favour of a taste for happiness... And yet, I own a *Descent from the Cross*, by Lorenzo Monaco, but the atmosphere of this painting is bathed in meditation, with no morbidity whatsoever. Christ is no longer there; his body looks almost transparent, and the elegance that emerges from the whole is very moving.

As for the idea of jubilation, it is primarily linked to the representation of the female body. If there are fewer art collectors in the Muslim world, I have often mused, it is surely because they have harems! Since I was unable to

ART

have my own harem, I have collected works of art... I passionately love the Picasso of his joyful periods. Thanks to the genius of his strokes, you can breathe in the physical happiness he must have experienced in 1932 for example, or in 1946, in 1969... These works are odes to sensuality in which young women are almost "innocently" erotic, surprised, calm, totally fresh... depicted from the front, in profile, from the back, relaxed in sleep or living a waking dream. To sleep near these paintings is a form of rapture.

When I was very young, I remember walking through museums and looking at the absolutely exquisite, naked female bodies that are so common in Western painting and which evoked indifference from the other visitors. "But they aren't really seeing anything!" I thought to myself. I was staggered that they didn't seem to appreciate the fantastically erotic side of what was right before their eyes. Because, for a man, the female nude is actually the most beautiful thing on earth, and the only sight one never grows weary of. And the fact that it is there, right in front of us, with no one, or almost no one, being filled with wonder is always incomprehensible to me.

Such elation can also be seen in a painting of an apple or a vase of flowers, but it is even more obvious when the painting is of a nude. I sometimes find myself dazzled by the curve of a neck, the way an ear joins the cheek, a budding breast or the hollow in the small of the back. Any part of the female body is capable of appearing as a sudden revelation, which painting continually reflects. When Géricault returned from England towards the end of his life, he painted the young wife of Colonel Bro, one of his friends with whom he stayed.

A TASTE FOR HAPPINESS

The scene is Montmartre, with Paris in the distance. Here is someone with the highest moral standards: her feet are crossed, her hands folded, her face somewhat tense. But you can make out the outline of her breasts beneath her very beautiful white dress, and they are freedom itself; they betray the carnal side of this woman, which is her true nature, a side of her that might even be unknown to herself. The sensitivity of the painter, whom we imagine is in love with her, is quite extraordinary. The combination of severity, even prudishness, mixed with a kind of sensuality that is discreetly revealed, provide a balance to the painting that makes this portrait one of the masterpieces of French painting. Nothing is heavy-handed; everything relies on nuance. Every time I look at this painting, my eyes are drawn to her bosom, which is completely covered and more than proper. You can sense a gift that is being denied, but it is a gift all the same: it is a marvellous painting.

Every so often, the way the body is posed, a certain gesture, or the placement of an arm or leg provide a feeling of certainty, perhaps even the very justification for the meaning of life.

There was a time when I refused to go to my office in Rockefeller Center until I had seen at least one very beautiful woman in the street. I would walk around below the buildings for five minutes. Fortunately, I have the joy of being able to block out certain things. I see only what is magnificent, nothing else. I become entranced, and the more scantily dressed people are, the more entranced I become. A naked woman is never ugly: a round little tummy delights me, a heavy breast can still be admired.

This is why spring and summer are a source of boundless pleasure to all men.

One of the principal impulses behind Western Art is eroticism and there can be no eroticism without individual characters. If Persian or Japanese miniatures are not very erotic, it's because they do not portray this type of being. I would make an exception for Indian bas-reliefs, perhaps because their eroticism contains a sense of *joie de vivre* that is apparent in the way the figures are positioned as a whole. Byzantine icons do not really move me because they do not portray any particular beings. This is the opposite of Early Renaissance Art from Siena and Florence; despite being very close in spirit to Byzantine Art, something very essential has taken place that changes everything: the individual can be seen beneath the prototype. After the beginning of the Renaissance, a Virgin Mary is no longer an image of the Virgin, she is a woman, a woman who loves, who suffers, who is anxious, tender, generous... An Annunciation by Fra Angelico is a mixture of grace and jubilation. The painter physically captures the beauty of the soul, Mary is already expecting her child, you can sense it in the way she holds herself.

The way beauty is revealed through a unique character marks the true beginning of what I love in Western Art, an art where one goes from the unique to the universal, not the other way around. For the same reason, the ancient arts – that deal in archetypes – leave me cold. I am not passionate about Egyptian Art, with rare exceptions, because I can sense a certain rejection of the individual in favour of the universal. In Greek sculpture, on the other hand, in spite of themselves and because they sought beauty for beauty's sake, their artists discarded the use of archetypes to achieve a way of representing people in all their diversity. And what I love most in Italy, often influenced by the Netherlands, is primarily a certain sense of moderation that reigned in Florence during the Renaissance, particularly in the frescos, which were my first love, and in which you find admirable restraint and timidity in the way people are portrayed. This moderation also exists in the works of Giotto, Masaccio and Masolino, with a balance in their simple colors, something that rejects any exaggeration or triviality. Venetian Art also delights me through a more generous display of flesh which painting alone can provide and which translates the internal complexity of human beings. Once the Baroque Period of the Counter-Reformation begins, I am less enthusiastic because I hardly appreciate the deliberate glorification of a particular cause, in this case, Catholicism, even if it is a just cause. The Italy that I love is the Italy of Bellini, of Raphael, of Botticelli...

Titian, of course, is an extraordinary genius and one of the best examples of how a painter improves with age. His later paintings become more and more ravishing, even his excesses become tolerable. He is no longer painting for others; he is painting for himself.

But when it is done for oneself, it is another manner. This reminds me of a formidable picture by Titian, *The Flaying of de Marsyas*. It is not intended to terrify the spectator; you can sense such spirituality in the work. Titian has painted it for himself, with unrivalled freedom, which lends beauty to this powerful image.) Antonello de Messine, one of my favourite painters, also paints horrific scenes of the suffering Christ, but in such a spiritual way that I am moved. He does not exaggerate suffering; he simply shows a man who suffers.

When the subject of a painting deals with meditations on death or depicts a form of brutality, excess, cynicism, deconstruction or borders on Expressionism. It becomes too distant for me to appreciate it. These are boundaries that I set; I do not enjoy all art: I enjoy what appeals to my soul. I would even dare go so far as to admit that there are entire periods of Italian Art that I do not like at all. Michelangelo's excesses do not please me because the transformation of the real into the surreal seems to me a betrayal of reality. And the most beautiful thing that can exist is reality. I admire the technique and virtuosity of Bernini but feel the same type of reluctance towards his work. I am therefore unable to say that Italy is my favourite country where art is concerned, but it is nevertheless the nation where art was founded, and with such a unique profusion of inventions and achievements that it is clearly impossible not to acknowledge it.

Nevertheless, I feel as happy with Flemish painters like Van Eyck, Van der Weyden or Memling, whom I admire just as much. Memling's Virgin Mary moves me: she is more secretive than affectionate with her child, who smiles and looks bright. In truth, Mary's tenderness speaks to all of mankind; she has been chosen by God and there exists within her a mixture of self-assurance and reserve that reveals great modesty. A so-called "still life" by Ambrosius Bosschaert depicting not only flowers, but also a dragonfly, a fly, a butterfly, makes an impression. They are not embellishments; each component has its own place in the universe. Everything contributes to providing a metaphysical element to the work of art with delicacy and with a certain power.

France has the good fortune of standing mid-way between these two influences, from the north and the south. I like places where tastes merge. Out of a kind of confusion, order is born. Amongst the early French masters is the "*Maître des Moulins*" whose work is inspired by Flanders. The Avignon Pietà, by the northern painter, Enguerrand Quarton, is inspired by Italy. In addition to these two poles in taste, add the influence of Greece, for its purity. Thanks to Greece, French taste became more refined; the Baroque or even Expressionist elements from Italy and Flanders were quickly removed. As a result, what follows is the feeling – one that perhaps is aligned to an idea rather than to a reality – that French Art is more objective than subjective: a type of art that leans toward a form of very sensitive detachment, in particular in the seventeenth century, as in the works of Poussin or Le Nain, artists who viewed reality with candor, while containing their emotions.

This attitude visible in French Art already exists in Gothic Art and, in a key way, in the thirteenth century, an exceptional century in France – in particular where the creation of Parisian art objects is concerned – a century during which Western Art attains its pinnacle. I found myself more and more interested in this period, a little by chance, when I decided to offer my help to the Cloisters and the Medieval department of the Metropolitan Museum of Art in New York, feeling that the public in the United States lacked an understanding of the Middle Ages. Along with

ART

the Early Renaissance, the Medieval Period is now the era I admire more than any other.

My grandfather also loved sharing his enjoyment of art, and did so whole-heartedly. One day, he gave the Louvre a pair of very rococo wine coolers by Thomas Germain which are, under any circumstance, masterpieces of French Art. They are, in my opinion, among the most beautiful examples of French silver because Germain, having attempted to create something baroque (rather unusual, given that he was an artist who normally produced classical works), succeeded in producing something perfectly French. In other words, these objects are an enormous fantasy and yet extremely restrained, both at the same time.

I like an object of art to have a kind of definition in space. It must be neither weak nor imprecise: it must be imposing, and its presence should be so strong that the artist's creative energy is concentrated in it. As soon as it overdone, it becomes less important. The difference between Greek and Roman sculpture is precisely that Roman sculpture is imprecise – it cannot be categorized – whereas Greek sculpture has a certain precision and density which were subsequently lost.

A great work of art stops you in your tracks, because, for just one instant, the entire world is captured in it. Every now and again, a work of art is perfectly precise: there is nothing that can be removed, nothing to add, it is exactly as it should be. Cistercian Art eliminated any embellishments or opulence, and if the Cistercian Abbeys like Sénanque or Le Thoronet move me, it is because they are imposing and necessary. They look as natural as the landscape in which they are perfectly integrated.

The subtle rigor of the French seventeenth century, with its choice of colors that dazzle through their clarity and boldness, the reds, blues, pure yellows of this period of painting also delight me. Human nature is never idealized in these works, as it is in Italian painting. A Virgin Mary by Fra Angelico is swathed in pure spirituality and that is obviously to be admired; a Madonna by Botticelli radiates the sublime. On the other hand, the Virgin painted by Mathieu Le Nain is a beautiful woman from France, very different from a Mediterranean Virgin. At her side, Joseph is a French peasant. He has lived, he understands. The baby in Mary's arms is independent of his mother, who, in this case, is more tired than sorrowful. We have this same impression in Poussin's painting *The Flight into Egypt*, which is called *The Flight with Elephant*, and whose subject I love immensely: his portrayal of the Virgin is eminently French, with a sensuous quality that allowed the artist to create his picture with the right touch of intimacy. You are looking in, but not intruding into this moment in the life of this young family, blessed as it is by the presence at its side of two graceful and beautiful angels. Mary and Joseph are being hunted down, little children are being killed, which is why they are leaving. And, suddenly, they stop: there is grace in life, happiness in being together; it is extraordinary.

Chardin, Watteau, Boucher and Fragonard are part of this French line. A bit of melancholy may creep in to certain paintings and, of course, a great deal of sensuality, but there is always a sense of discretion. This is actually why I object so strongly to German Art: very early on and simultaneously, it took on Expressionism and a kind of violence. If, in my opinion, Ingres is the greatest French master of the nineteenth century, it is because he demonstrates, almost to the point of caricature, the desire for objectivity in French Art. There is an obvious coldness, often a certain detachment, not always, but even in his very sensual paintings, one senses that he sees from a distance.

I am very mindful of the way Impressionism expresses joy in the world, whether a painting by Monet or Renoir, and in the works that followed, for example, Cézanne's attempts to recreate a sense of order. It was not completely successful – as he was well aware – but very moving. Cézanne constantly tried to refocus perspective to try to better approach reality, and I am very sensitive to that. Just as I am equally fond of the last spurt of French Art, the last up to now, but not the very last, at least we hope not, with Picasso, whom I consider far more French than Spanish, to the extent that he never loses control. Even when he is painting something like *Guernica*, he doesn't let himself go off into some sort of lyricism; he is restrained, and that is what is beautiful, what is moving and what links him to what I call French Art. He is steeped in restraint, even when he is depicting the violence of the world. Picasso's *Dora Maar* is the portrait of a woman in pain who is crying, but this painting is not over-exaggerated. With Bacon or Basquiat, however, the excessive becomes the painting, while with Picasso, it is portrayed, but at a distance. And, of course, Matisse is heir to a school of happiness in the French style.

Even if the painters I like are far from being uniquely French, they must not be in opposition to my taste for what is French in order for me to fully appreciate them. And this is why I am enthusiastic about geniuses like Rembrandt, Rubens, Raphael, Titian, Velasquez. It is with Dürer, El Greco, Caravaggio that I begin to have more problems... Because they have no detachment, they attempt to express themselves powerfully, without restraint, and yet this is what is admired in their works today. But, since I am not a complete rigorist, I can also be moved by a painting that almost entirely contradicts everything I think, simply because it is beautiful. El Greco's View of Toledo during a storm is an indisputable masterpiece, yet one that does not entirely conform to what I profess to admire; I am simply overwhelmed by his talent. Caravaggio is not one of my favourite painters; he is far too expressionistic for my taste and yet, in his magnificent still lives in particular, the joy of life bursts forth. Goya isn't a favourite either and, even if his inspiration is foreign to me, I find certain of his works admirable, for example, his painting of the little boy in red that hangs in the Metropolitan.

Velasquez's works are far more beautiful... Why? When I look at the study he made for the figure of Apollo in the *The Forge of Vulcan*, a great work he did in Rome, I find an incomparable stylistic freedom: the profile is almost blurred, you cannot tell where he is looking, his curly hair is dishevelled, he has that southern complexion, all bronzed, and he looks as if he is moving... In fact, he looks like a young girl, but he is actually a boy from the streets of Rome in the seventeenth century, painted with the rapid rhythm of his turbulent youth, very touching. All of the painter's fantastic talent is concentrated in this sketch: his authority is undisputed; there is not a moment of weakness, it is striking in its perfection. Here is something so prominent that we believe we have encountered the Art of Painting.

French paintings are not always the most beautiful in the world but they are the ones whose inspirations best corresponds to my definition of art, like a personal interpretation of the world and of people, that retains the essence of their souls, without seeking to misrepresent in order to impress. I want art to take me deeper into a well-ordered world, one that corresponds to my desire for a certain idyllic world, perhaps a bit artificial, but desirable, a world where it is possible to unite the heart and the mind in unique understanding, where the friction between horror and admiration, between disorder and enchantment disappears, and where it is possible to construct what man has always sought to construct, or so it seems to me, that is, a sense of order that is favourable to man. Beauty may exist elsewhere, and it is almost a question of nature: I prefer a calm sea to a raging sea, fields of wheat in summer to a landscape of rocks deformed by the wind. I like expressions of man's long effort to adapt the world in a way that might give him joy.

If I am so sensitive to French taste, this is because it displays a true desire for beauty and elegance, balance, a lack of excess and respect for the painting's subject. There is a magnificence that is French. What strikes me in eighteenth century paintings by Fragonard, Watteau, Boucher, Nattier, Lancret, Natoire and many others, is that all their women look intelligent. They do not paint likeable idiots, but spiritual beauties. They arouse happiness: they

A TASTE FOR HAPPINESS

are subtle, ravishing, gracious, delicious... And through them passes the very bustle of life for life's sake, lively, sparkling, joyous. They all look different, and they are all delectable. Take, for example, Watteau's young woman who is flirting: you can see the hesitation on her face, partly fear, partly amusement, partly desire, partly acceptance, and it is she who places her lover's hand on her breast. Here we have the world of tenderness and humanity that once existed and is completely evoked: it is there, right before our eyes. But who sees it?

Fragonard and Watteau are still appreciated... But these days, almost no one values Boucher: too many curves, too soft, too much whipped cream! It seems almost embarrassing to find him interesting. Such enthusiasm seems pointless, his brilliance doesn't catch our attention, his mastery leaves us outraged. Boucher is accused of being bland, a lightweight and, fundamentally, so French, and yet, he is a painter whom I passionately love. A pleasant work of art is considered to be easy. But what does it mean to call a work difficult? That it is arduous or that its subject is so painful that no one has any desire whatsoever to linger over it?

An American art critic damned Boucher when he declared, with amazing scorn and hypocrisy, that he was "an advocate of soft pornography", which, coming from a puritanical spirit of today, surrounded by hard pornography that no longer shocks anyone, is rather ironic. He would never have dared say such a thing about the Venus de Milo or Velasquez's famous nude. To tell the truth, the main crime of Boucher's painting is that it expresses pleasure. Boucher gets too carried away in order to celebrate the joy of being alive and in such an obvious way that his painting becomes embarrassing. To certain people – and to the majority of my contemporaries I am sorry to say – the flights of fancy evoked by too many flowers in full bloom, too many richly textured fabrics, too many laughing children and too many delectable women are unbearable, which speaks volumes about their state of mind. But Boucher is a genius. And, like all geniuses, he recreates reality. He sees the world on a large scale, he varies his formats and his subjects; he is a master of his art. Where color, shape, material, bodies, figures and drawing are concerned, he has proved himself exceptional. He has not only set himself the goal of becoming competent in all these elements when capturing space, color and drawing, but he also attains it. Most people prefer violence and chaos to pastoral or romantic scenes. Well, that's a shame; as for me, I always make sure that I go and see my Boucher paintings, studying them one by one with great pleasure, as I do with all my paintings, whether they are French or not, whenever I come home, to New York or somewhere else. And the fact that all this beauty exists brings me great comfort.

What pleases me a great deal in French Art – and I am thinking in particular now about the still lives by Chardin and Monet, or Corot's landscapes – is its respect for everyday objects, like saucepans, tables or tablecloths, or a country scene, a port, flowers, and the peaceful domestication of nature, which does not preclude sensuality. In various scenes in Corot's works, one senses the harshness of life, but also the dignity of the peasants and the affection of the painter. The French only understand nature as tame and re-made by man. Moreover, the French do not prevaricate, there is nothing covered up; there is honesty in their gaze. This is one of the elements that make France a flesh and blood country, unlike the Scandinavian countries or America, where everything is watered down, where people only desire things that do not appear to be what they really are. I find this hopeless desire to hide the reality of our true needs shocking. In France, all parts of an animal can be food, everything is eaten and... it is all exposed. The deliciously ripe autumn fruits, the flowers that Delacroix painted in springtime for Georges Sand, with whom he was in love, speak of his desire subtly but openly and without sentimentality, and in abundance. And if French painters have greatly admired Flemish and Italian painting, they have loved it with their eyes and their taste, which, for me, makes it even more charming.

What brings me close to despair today is the existence of what might be called an aversion to French Art, which began with the defeat of France in May 1940. When that happened, the world lost its taste for France.

Everything we currently seem to appreciate clashes with French taste. All of Expressionism – German in particular – everything that is High Baroque, seventeenth century Italian painting, the School of Naples, where the art of irony and exaggeration enjoyed great success, practically all contemporary art – is completely out of step with what I love – all this is, in consequence, anti-French and for this I reproach them the most! The most serious thing of all is that the French themselves took up this idea and so French artists no longer produce French Art. They lost their inspiration, but actually, this all happened fairly recently – Matisse only died about fifty years ago, Picasso, about thirty years ago – and they were both

ART

part of this school, Matisse completely, Picasso a great deal, but ever since, artists have turned their backs and are moving in a totally different direction.

Official French Art, which exists, unfortunately – the art of the FRAC (*Fonds régionaux d'art contemporain*), the kind of art often praised by the Minister of Culture and curators of modern art museums – is greatly suspicious of French taste. And everything that resembles French Art is mocked the world over. Pajou, a French sculptor of the eighteenth century, is most highly esteemed when he seems to be Italian, that is to say, more expressionist than he normally is. The Metropolitan in New York recently acquired a statue by Pajou, bought in Paris, and at great cost. Moreover, it was the only one in the entire sale that did not look French. And, thanks to the power of the herd instinct, it was admired above all the others. They paid six times more for a statue by an eminently French sculptor, because it didn't appear to be French. "That statue is very beautiful," I said to the curator, but it doesn't really look French." "How right you are!" he replied, delighted.

That such a thing would happen was inevitable. French Art had been dominant for more than two hundred years. From a historical perspective, it must therefore seem somewhat normal for people's taste to change. Even more so since, at the beginning of the twentieth century, with Marie Laurencin and certain other painters from the School of Paris, the idea of French Art deteriorated and fell into the notion of creating something "pretty for pretty's sake". Nevertheless, there were still some important, beautiful creations by artists, like Bonnard, for example, some of whose work I like, but not most, as he often paints on a small scale... little interiors, little scenes, all of it is very limited, with rare exceptions!... like the wonderfully erotic painting of a young woman seen from the back, yellow in the bright sun... which lights up the entrance hall of my house in the Midi.

The first converts to the hatred of French Art were French artists themselves. And such hatred remains without equal in the world. Spanish painters, like Tàpies or Barcelo, Italian painters, like Clemente, and even German painters whose taste I do not admire, like Baselitz or Kiefer, remain faithful to their tradition. In France, this is not the case, perhaps with the exception of Pierre Soulages or François Rouan. Hence this tremendous decline in French Art.

And yet, people have not really changed. They experience the same feelings of joy when presented with beauty, the same emotions when they sense tenderness, the same exhilaration before intelligence, but what is sad is that they no longer believe that all those emotions are a part of art. Art must shock people into seeing the world in all its violence. The result of this idea is that we are seeing the success of an artistic subculture, that is to say second rate art, whose purpose is to fill in the void created left by the absence of artistic beauty. Perhaps we are coming to the end of this cycle in France, but we have lived through a period of fifty years when there have been attempts to sweep away a French aesthetic, and this has had disastrous consequences for the nation. By losing a sense of what is beautiful, we have denied an entire part of our personality. One of the foundations of French pride has vanished; and because of this, we are no longer capable of integration, and not only where foreigners are concerned. At the heart of any nation, individuals can confirm their identify, or not, through certain number of values of which they are proud. French taste was one such value, but it is no longer the case.

Today, art is taught at school by teachers who often are not familiar with French Art. Recently, at the *Académie des beaux-arts*, I attended a very interesting discussion on this subject. Several people agreed that there was an entire generation of teachers who were no longer in touch with their culture. One of those attending, a former professor, then took the floor. He said he was convinced that everything he had taught was of no interest and had not actually served any purpose, in the sense that each person had to discover his own idea of beauty, and that; as a result, learning anything at all would have no influence. To which the filmmaker Roman Polanski replied that if "we could not teach how to love, we could at least teach how to make love", an idea I found very appealing.

During the 1930s, France was still at the cutting edge for all painters. This is no longer the case; the Americans have their own painters and are attracting others. Add to this the fact that the more powerful a country is, the more valuable its art becomes, as the leading art collectors are natives. We must remember this aspect, since it is an integral factor in the world of art. American Art is therefore more highly esteemed than Spanish art Art, and I am giving this example intentionally, because Spanish Art is recognized – it is not worthless.

In addition, there is the pure and simple phenomenon of what is in fashion. And what is fashionable in itself remains rather mysterious. People choose their homes in a certain way: today, they like large, empty white spaces. Add a painting by Boucher and it is out of place. They need paintings with strong colors and simple shapes. Moreover, since the end of the nineteenth century, professional people are so terribly afraid of being behind the times that they value the innovative element in a work of art, placing it above what one might expect. They say over and over again: "This painting launched such and such an idea, or allowed the creation of a particular school..." Immediately, that painting becomes much more expensive than another, which might be more beautiful, because it is "innovative". This phenomenon of being in fashion also affects museums as they are extraordinarily afraid of being left by the wayside. Having experienced, second-hand, so to speak, the academicism of the beginning of the century, which was blind to the Impressionist school, to Van Gogh and Gauguin, I see museums panicking over the idea that they do not understand what is happening. And so museums have recreated a new academicism consisting of constant splits and innovations that are sometimes devoid of meaning. One must always do something different, be prepared to be persuaded to negate, to the point of destroying the very idea of art itself. What's more, we should recognize, I believe, that there is no progression in art and I dispute any concept of a linear history of art. The supremacy of the innovative contributes to the creation of a fashion and, as a result, creates rather serious imbalances.

There is another current trend, which seems obvious to us but which has not always been so evident: a work of art that is not attributed to any major painter has little value. Here is a magnificent painting by an unknown artist: no buyers. A still life by Caravaggio will fetch extravagant sums, but a still life by the Hartford Master, who is perhaps the very person who painted all of Caravaggio's still lives, are worth much less because it is not signed by Caravaggio. The absurdity of this attitude reaches its peak where furniture is concerned. Thanks to my grandfather, I learned not to attach great importance to the signature on a piece of furniture. If I found something beautiful and it was from eighteenth century, it was of little importance whether it was signed by Carlin or not. Today, a piece of furniture that is not signed is worth a great deal less than one whose maker is known. Moreover, it is important to realize that many makers' marks are in circulation and are easy to copy. And so, all of this is in vain, yet it does not prevent such criteria being used as the basis for differences in price.

In addition, scarcity makes an object or painting more valuable. The National Gallery in London held a work by Raphael in trust; the owner wished to sell it, and the museum made desperate attempts to keep it.

Now, it is not that the museum does not own any Raphaels; it probably has more beautiful ones, but the main reason they wanted this one was because there are no more Raphaels in private collections. They are all in museums, so when one turns up, even if it is not basically that important, it is still very valuable.

When works of art are not valuable, they are never seen, because they remain in private collections. I remember a sale in New York, a long time ago, when some Millets were sold for high prices. Millet was an artist who was then associated with the academic painters and his works were never to be found. Now, that sale caused a shock: people suddenly understood that Millet was actually an artist. And, overnight, his paintings came on the market, but at very high prices. I was not tempted, even though I recognize that Millet is a valid artist. On the other hand, Pompon, the French animal sculptor of the 1920s and 30s, whose work I admire, is still poorly thought of, unless the work resembles a Bugatti; and, if it is less smooth than usual, more anguished, and therefore in fashion, it will be eight times more expensive. Ten years ago, Pompon's works were never seen, while presently, they are re-surfacing. Where furniture is concerned, I have never liked royal pieces intended for display. They have lost their sincerity out of a desire to arouse admiration; they exist to impress. They are affected and, as a result, there is something about them that is unsatisfying.

An object can be sumptuous, but it must appear to be subtle. I am thinking of the most beautiful fireplace I have ever seen.

It is said to have belonged to Madame du Barry and was in the château of Louveciennes when Japanese speculators acquired it, then sold it to dealers from whom I bought it. It is rectangular, made of white marble, gilt, and graceful. You can imagine it in an elegant room in Paris, but not at Versailles. I still have a Louis XVI desk that belonged to my father; it is well-proportioned and unostentatious. While it does have small gilt-bronze mounts at the corners, they are not there to impress, but rather simply to highlight the purity of the desk's lines. The armchair that goes with it belonged to my grandfather: its deep redwood color, the fact that it is beautiful from every perspective, adorned without being heavy, all these things show a taste for quality and refinement, without the need to overdo. That is why I love it, just as I love things that appear to be different from what they are. Certain Louis XVI chairs, for example, look English even though they are French, from a time when everyone admired the English style.

My taste for French art goes so far as to define my relationship with the world. It has always provided me with a tendency toward happiness... One can influence people to be happy, at least for a while, though, sadly, not indefinitely. Given the desire to attain a certain balance, people can be compelled to act and behave as if they believed in happiness, all the while knowing that at the slightest momentary weakness or weariness, unhappiness is always laying in wait, and will come crashing down on you. When that happens, you must either recover your strength or flee. One cannot simply sit still and endure an invasion of chaos caused by a sort of indulgence toward unhappiness.

To be surrounded by works of art is very helpful. I draw on the perspective of artists whose works correspond to my own intentionally well-ordered view of the world to provide me with the means necessary to prevent an avalanche. To me, art is the reference point for the proper way of seeing the world. To visually immerse myself in a universe of beauty, joy, respect and elegance renews my awareness that to be demanding is a good thing, and that one must not allow oneself to give in to the temptation of disorder. I refuse to, which explains why certain people in the business world find me harsh, but I do not wish to allow myself to be dragged down into chaos. If there is no distance between yourself and other people, the slightest disruptive influence from someone else can affect you. If the impact is not very strong and you keep yourself at a distance, it will not harm you. And, when doubt sometimes manages to creep in, going home, studying a painting or object of art and reminding myself once more that beauty exists, is essential in the battle that I wage every day, not only to be respected, but, what is perhaps even more important, to have the ability to respect others. If the day comes when people can no longer respect each other, something will have seriously broken down.

I accept that there is an art of disorder, of violence, of irony, but such visions leave me cold. Other worlds exist which I might, perhaps, have to bear, but they are not my worlds. While I may have to be surrounded by what is unpleasant, I do not associate with it. I am not interested in death; too many people are fascinated by it. And this morbid tendency, which is an essential element in contemporary art, those horrible photographs, and sinister installations are not really appealing to me. Not only do I find them boring, but I think that if you expect the best it has more chance of happening than if you expect the worst. Bad feelings only engender more bad feelings; there is no guaranty that good feelings will only give rise to more good feelings, but it is a pleasant attitude in itself, and probably more useful.

The world is not perfect and, insofar as it is possible, it is essential to attempt to exclude violence from life. This attitude almost sounds like white magic and, of course, it is never wholly possible to manage it; nevertheless, it is not completely impossible, if luck is on your side.

My idea of beauty is not consistent with ruin. On the contrary, it has to do with a miracle which, through its form and inspiration, reveals one moment captured in time and lovingly recreates it. This sensation can be found beyond art, but there is a difference: in art, it is recreated, while in life, on the other hand, it is recreated but then lost again... It can be captured again at times, but in art, it is always there. Sometimes, just one detail is sufficient: take the scene with Vermeer's little yellow wall in Proust's *À la Recherche du temps perdu*. Its very existence transports you... And yet, my vision of art is not an escape from the world but a deepening of what I love in the universe, a taste for beauty that exists in all civilisations since the short time when men became sufficiently well-off to have the leisure to do something other than merely survive.

I do not believe much in the permanence of things, nor in success, nor in attaining any goals; nor do I believe in progress or the uniqueness of the human race; I do not believe in the afterlife yet, at the same time, I contradict myself because I recognize that art is unique to man. It is the one permanent feature of humanity and, when all is said and done, the only thing that sets us apart. Almost everything else seems to me, and I say this with no intention to criticize whatsoever, part of the animal world, and I find this perfectly respectable. It is inconceivable to me to think there is an essential difference between our existence and the existence of animals: I have come to terms with the fact that I am an animal. What sets us apart is the ability to create beauty, which by its very nature is fleeting, through a work of art that is inherently more permanent. To me, this takes the place of spirituality, perhaps by default.

All such testaments to the past are very moving. A certain expression of faith, of joie de vivre, or the ability to transform everyday objects, all these things are part of our lives, whether they succeed or fail, because there are, of course, many works of art, even important ones, that are clumsy. I have no desire whatsoever to break away from this universe where pivotal eras and ages are reflected. Art also geographically reflects a particular spirit from a given region at one moment in time, accompanied, moreover, by the total mystery of talent or genius that is never demonstrated so well as when artists are commissioned to paint specific subjects. In a certain way, this has allowed painters to come into their own, because their subjects are dictated, which gives them more freedom. When there are choices, a lot of time is lost on wondering what to paint.

And that is a waste of time because what matters most is not what one is going to paint, but the way in which it will be done. The Virgin and Child has been painted a hundred thousand times, but there are only a thousand that are masterpieces. Why? This is an almost impenetrable mystery, and one that the artist himself would be unable to explain, though it is a part of him. When Rembrandt painted himself dressed as a wealthy young man, he portrayed himself as "stylish", and yet it shows marvellous talent. He has a sweet expression and he knows he is a great painter, but that isn't his fault!

The work of art is of prime importance, and it is often enhanced by the humility of the artist. It is not by chance that painters who are inspired by great faith are often major artists, because they are modest where their work is concerned. Little is known about Fra Angelico; Rembrandt's life can be explained; but what counts in both cases is their work. In Velasquez or Raphael, the urge to create beauty is more powerful in the artist than what he brings to the subject, and you can feel that they would do anything, including self-effacement, in order to attain it. Every time I sense that attitude, I am more deeply affected by it. My taste is strangely led along a certain path. In the same way, even though I might admire the Goya of the final years, when he wanted to prove something – the horror of war, to be specific – I cannot prevent myself from thinking that any attempt to involve oneself, even in the name of a good cause, only results in something second rate. It may not be unimportant, but it is not essential. I believe far more in necessity and the virtue of personal detachment in order to create something miraculous.

Has art replaced God in my life? Yes and no... There is no salvation in art, and nothing is eternal. Anyone who believes he possesses very ancient works of art, is wrong. If we agreed to measure time in terms of the eighty years of human life, everything is still relatively recent. A painting by Corot is the equivalent of two human lifetimes, and the two lions that are part of a Moorish chess set that I like very much, is the equivalent of ten human lifetimes, which is not that old: it takes us back to the twelfth century. A little painting that is one of the oldest in France dates from 1400, six hundred years, so eight human lifetimes... All these works of art are rather new and, whether humanity survives for a long time or not, they will disappear. The human race is in its early stages and it is very difficult to know if it will endure. It is a question of one epiphenomenon linked to the other epiphenomenon that is our own existence. It is pointless to exaggerate the importance of this: it is only important to us! We are a species that is destined to disappear and a man's life does not last very long. And so, make the most of it! The series of chance events that made our world possible is fascinating: the fact that we have an air to breathe, that our atmosphere is so thin, that there is a moon which is essential to keeping our planet in equilibrium... All these things happened fortuitously, and believing that we are an eternal species at the center of the universe is astounding to me. In reality, everything encourages me to try to enjoy the good fortune we have of living on a planet that is so disconcertingly fragile.

The fact that Watteau exists, that Velasquez exists... all this, in and of itself, is a great source of joy. And also the fact that the world is so beautiful: there is life, trees, grass, and it all quivers with motion... Standing in front of a certain landscape, one can recognize a Dutch or Italian painting. Seeing a certain face, one is transported back to a magical French portrait from the eighteenth century. That all these things exist provides me with another reason to be happy. We are all going to die, but death is not the true mystery, the true mystery is life. Now people might know very well that they are going to die, yet they behave just as animals do, without a true awareness of their own mortality. It is something that does not come into the workings of everyday life. When all is said and done, if there were no children, one could say that in fifty years, there would be no one left alive. This is nothing to be afraid of, no one has a choice in the matter, and this fact consoles me enormously. Death is nothing. It may be mysterious, but it is not very important. We have all seen an animal die: it was there, then it was not, that's all there is to it. I do not see anything in that to make a horrible fuss about. What is sad about seeing a person die is that both his knowledge and experience disappear. But that is also almost true of animals: every animal is unique, and this individuality is a loss. The similarities between the species seem to me far superior to the few differences that exist between man and animals. I know that saying this might sound shocking, but I truly think that we are animals: we have evolved a bit more perhaps, but then again, not always!

Behind every work of art there is an artist, who is either dead or will die one day, but the work of art or the painting will last a bit longer, because at least we have the ability to feel the environment, the emotion, the way of seeing the world that the artist felt. The original intention might sometimes be misconstrued or difficult to perceive because of our taste or lack of culture, but this is not a serious problem because what endures is the talent that has been passed on through an individual at a certain moment in time. The artist is not always remembered; he might not have been terribly interesting; no one accurately recalls the kind of life he led, but he had a gift that was passed on. To a certain extent, I have always had a slight reservation when an artist's personality and talent were merged. For a long time, I did not really love two painters who are incredibly in vogue today, Van Gogh and Gauguin, precisely because it is so difficult to disentangle the artist from his work. To me, the works were spoiled because of this. When I look at a painting by Gauguin, I cannot help thinking of Gauguin the man, and that troubles me. When I went to see the Gauguin exhibition in Paris, I found that the paintings were enhanced by being all together because, strangely enough, even today, I still feel a certain uneasiness when I look at them individually, a feeling I would qualify as the touristy element of the works. The exhibition allowed me to grasp the fantastic colors that appear in all the paintings, but the element of translating Polynesian culture into a Christian framework, which pleases Westerners, nevertheless seems rather unpleasantly distorted. It reveals an art that is falsely Polynesian and falsely Christian and it is very successful, even if I am a bit shocked by the process. I have a rather similar feeling towards Van Gogh; his depiction of madness displeases me, because it has a personal element which, to my eyes, takes something away from the work of art. Nonetheless, when I look at his paintings and drawings of Provence, which are marvellous, and see it as Van Gogh saw it, true sincerity emerges in his relationship with nature, something I do not feel with Gauguin when he paints Tahiti.

Taste is formed, and grows. This is one of the two privileges of age, along with the physical awkwardness that is forgivable when one reaches seventy, but not before, even though I have always been congenitally clumsy! To climb onto a horse, I have always needed a little stepladder. At the age of twenty-three, such a thing is ridiculous; at my age, it is respectable. One of the great joys in growing older is that everything that has always been now seems normal. The other joy is that you continue to have experiences, so you never stop learning. And since art is so incredibly diverse, not a day goes by when I do not learn something about an artist or a school of painting.

The ability to see the relationship between different objects of art interests me enormously. When I went to Brazil and saw some Baroque statues, a great expert on Brazil and its art told me that I had made the same observations as Germain Bazin, an authority on Brazilian Baroque Art. I find it very amusing when my instinctive reaction proves to be knowledgeable. The other day, in New York, I was shown a magnificent thirteenth century Virgin Mary from Paris; she was made of ivory and wore a metal crown on her head. That crown bothered me and I asked if it was part of the original piece. They told me it wasn't: the Virgin Mary was part of a group and it was originally the angel next to her who had worn the crown.

At the end of the nineteenth century, as often happened, the group was broken up, and the crown ended up on the Virgin's head. I was rather pleased to have felt instinctively – thanks to that sum of knowledge which surges forth – that it was out of place. This Virgin would have been far more beautiful without that embellishment. When one begins to have a feel for quality and the relationship of things among themselves, this brings great pleasure. What also brings pleasure is having long ago shaken off the touching but annoying religious worship of works of art. Buying religious art, moreover, helps to remove its sacred aura.

One cannot love art if one is like a calf in his own pasture. It is necessary to delve into all components of the world of art. One of these components is its price, and this has always been so. You cannot cook if you don't get your hands dirty and, in the same way, you cannot totally understand art if you do not look at it through the eyes of the market. An object of art is not only a piece of merchandise, but it is also a piece of merchandise. The fact that it has a price, whether it is too expensive or not expensive enough, absurd or not, gives the object a more physical reality. Prices always fluctuate, and they change completely according to prevailing taste and when they are sold. No one can totally escape this fact, nor should anyone consider himself more knowledgeable than the times in which he lives. I look at art catalogues every day, and in all fields, including those in which I never buy. But when I see a painting that has a certain charm and for which extravagant sums are asked, it is obvious to me that something is not right. The opposite is also true. I was tempted to buy a painting by Jordaens, because it was relatively inexpensive, but I didn't purchase it in the end because it wasn't sufficiently appealing. From the point of view of the evolution of taste, however, it is nevertheless interesting. It cost ten times less than a bad Impressionist picture and a hundred times less than a good one; it wasn't an enormous amount for a recognized painting, and one that had probably belonged to Rubens.

One of the joys that comes with first becoming knowledgeable is being able to say, whether rightly or not: "That is very ugly" about an object or painting that many other people might admire, simply because it does not in any way appeal to your own taste. Ever since I was a child, I have hated a picture by Rembrandt – some man wearing a gold helmet – that is in Berlin. I was delighted to learn that the Rembrandt committee had decided that he hadn't painted it. They might be wrong, and I as well, but I immediately felt that this painting did nothing for me. I am also just as pleased when I do not like something as when I do. Of course, some things are very easy to dislike, if they are totally ugly, ineffectual, tampered with, insincere. But not liking a painting that is considered very beautiful by other people seems to me as liberating as passionately loving a work of art which is truly striking. I nearly bought a picture painted because of a particular event: someone's son gave all his money to a courtesan and then committed suicide after sleeping with her. But the way she was portrayed was rather dubious. By buying it, one becomes somewhat complicit in that. It displeased me; there was something false about it. It is the same when certain horrific sights arouse excitement: we cloak ourselves in a moralistic attitude as we eagerly look at them. In this respect, many Orientalist paintings are unbearable, while Delacroix's *La Mort de Sardanapale* is a real work of art. It contains all the ingredients of academic painting but the degree of honesty with which he portrays the human body saves this picture. In other works, the faces are rather unclear, the slaves are naked, but not completely, the artist does not follow the thought to its conclusion, and one has the impression that it is all an illusion. And I have never liked stories that are not true...

Capturing true beauty always seems to me unique. I make it my own and each person can do the same. All you have to do is look. This is true of architecture, painting, sculpture, the decorative arts. Indisputably, certain artists are gifted with powerful, creative inspiration, and others are not. This does not prevent them from creating wonderful paintings, but they will always be lacking genius. Because often, though not always, a great artist can show signs of genius in an average painting. And strangely enough, in an excellent painting by an average artist, this is lacking, quite simply because there is no genius. Thus, a painting works on two different levels: the painting itself and the evocative power of the genius...

It is essential to retain the ability to be surprised and take care that one's eye does not make anything seem banal, otherwise, all is lost. What is pitiful in mediocrity is that it dulls the senses. And the great privilege of seeing beautiful things every day is that they are constantly stimulating. I am continually delighted by the things I see which, far from distancing me from reality, allow me to perceive truth.

Unfortunately, most people today are blind and our senses have been dulled. If you are standing in the middle of a lush meadow in Normandy, you feel nothing any more. You need to be in a blazing hot desert, or among the rocks of a lunar landscape to experience something again. Our sensitivity has been weakened. This sometimes also happens to me: I do not hate it when I find myself in a swamp, but I reproach myself for it, as it is truly proof that my perception has been blunted and that I no longer feel what I should be feeling.

At the beginning of the nineteenth century, all the European painters made the famous journey to Italy, in order to soak up its natural beauty and restrained landscapes. And then, suddenly, they stopped. Not a single painter today makes the journey, and the result is that there is no longer a painter in residence at the Villa Medici in Rome, as incredible as that might seem. It is puzzling. And what does Barcelo, a painter whom I admire, paint? The desert, a watering hole in Africa...

Even though I know nothing about music, I was struck by a remark made by a musician of the *Académie des beaux-arts* who said that, before allowing his students to begin to work, he made them sit in silence for ten minutes, adding: "What is annoying about today's world is that you can hear nothing because there is too much noise." It is the same in painting: there is so much visual commotion that we only see the things that jump out at us. We are so used to strong colors, intense drawings, fantastical sounds and blinding lights that our sensitivity is affected. I too sometimes find such feverish excitement pleasing, but I am fortunate in that such din and bustle are the exceptions in my life, while most of my contemporaries cannot escape, they continually live within that world which changes the way they see life. So human beings are cut off from their own feelings, which explains the popularity of voyages to exotic places. However, I do believe that beauty is eternal, in a certain way, eternal on a human scale, and one which we must learn to see again. Even professionals are solely interested in things that arouse the maximum emotion and, consequently, in things that are obtrusive. And what is more obtrusive than horror? We are all guilty of this: we might not wish to look at something horrible, but it is difficult not to. If someone shows you a photo of an accident, it is very difficult to look away. This is how it is: horror stirs and emerges all by itself. Without going that far, an Expressionist painting – which expresses a state of mind, and not only the contemplation of or respect for what exists – might appear attractive to many people.

To me, a great painting is always a revelation and arouses feelings of freedom and joy. Standing in front of a nude by Titian or Velasquez, an Annunciation by Fra Angelico, one sees something perfectly obvious, something which does not need to be described or thought about, and which cannot be improved upon or altered because it is true. Now, we spend our lives seeking the moment when reality becomes beauty itself. And sometimes, when we look at a sky, or the sea or a person, we feel a profound sense of joy, of connection. The fact that painting offers us this feeling of completeness so totally and at any given moment is wondrous!

It is a wondrous thing that marks milestones and makes life considerably better.

But even though desire, passion and even tenderness are omnipresent in the pictorial world, I have believed for a long time that painting was incapable of depicting love, perhaps because love does not exist... If you take away affection and desire, and attempt to define love apart from these two qualities, what remains? A kind of flu, a fever! Perhaps this is why people turn away from painting and towards music, which is more skilful at expressing the abstract, while visual representation, by definition, is more analytical. Only music, which I rarely appreciate however, thus seems to me capable of incorporating the emotion of love. Certain passages where the singer breathes in between two arias by Mozart are very moving, the end of *La Traviata*, while indisputably grandiloquent, provide a convincing reality to the expression of love. But if love, like art, does exist, then yes, certain masterpieces in painting, because they exist, are love itself.

Their virtues surpass us but I have the feeling that, by loving them, it is possible to partially capture them. If I was so happy to have acquired those two lions from the twelfth century chess set, it is because I was lacking an example of the Arab-Andalusian civilisation. It is the same for the Virgin from 1400 that comes from the Île-de-France. French paintings from that period are rare and I immediately realized that this Virgin incarnated an extraordinarily desirable element of my spiritual family. To have it by my side, not forever, but at least for a while, is bliss.

Why did I desire to create a collection? No particular reason... it is the expression of a kind of *joie de vivre*, it is ephemeral. This is part of my family's tradition, but I live it as a personal adventure. It is a question of harmonizing objects and paintings that I love. I consider myself far more a lover of art than a collector of art. By definition, a collector is a kind of dictionary, he wishes to own different examples of talent from an era or painter. I am a lover of art, someone who truly loves art. Proust once said that art was the only way to see through someone else's eyes. This is a very appealing idea which explains the passion of the art lover, for there is no end to the joy of seeing through someone else's eyes. To be able to do this over and over again is so special that there is no reason to ever grow weary of it. One might possibly grow tired of the way in which one sees personally, but the ability to see through someone else's eyes is unique.

The idea that someone's taste – mine, in this instance – sheds a particular light on the world of art, delights me. To be surrounded by works of art is an attempt to introduce beauty, to integrate it effortlessly into daily life, without worrying about proving anything. You are surrounded by the rhythm, the contrast, the harmonious alliance between different objects. There is a physical resonance in space, the works of art are never abstract, and they are always evolving beneath each other's gaze. I am very fond of the idea that they all have histories associated with their own destinies. There are two paintings by Pieter De Hooch of a courtyard that still exists in Delft; in each, the painter has positioned his characters differently and they are, in my opinion, the two most beautiful paintings he ever created. Tranquillity gently falls onto this little courtyard, a weapon has been left at the entrance, life is lived to the full here, and at a leisurely pace: it is the triumph of the bourgeoisie at its most peaceful; one feels safe there; it is charming.

I am not like certain fetishist collectors who worship art because of who owned it. Nevertheless, I do like the idea of sharing the taste of someone who had good taste. It pleases and interests me a great deal that this painting by Pieter de Hooch had once belonged to Joséphine de Beauharnais. First, because I like her taste. Was she influenced by Vivant Denon? She was one of his friends, his mistress perhaps, in any case, she was the one who introduced him to Bonaparte. She was always a person who made very sophisticated choices, both old and new, since, on the one hand, she commissioned Redouté's roses and flowers that are amongst the most beautiful engravings of the period and because, on the other hand, she launched a style of art, rather minor, "troubadour" painting, which depicts the Middle Ages in a charming, though false way. And so Joséphine supported the art of her time, while simultaneously maintaining the delicacy of the *Ancien Régime*. This can be seen in a rug she had copied from the original, one of which is at Malmaison: ravishing pastel colors, perfectly harmonious.

It is much lighter and brighter than the Empire style, but it is new and of exceptional quality.

Like Choiseul, I love gilt-mounted porcelain vases. And I am delighted to own certain objects that used to belong to him, infinitely more than if they had been owned by Louis XIV, because Choiseul was an art collector whose taste I admire. He was extremely wealthy, as was his wife, but he ended up penniless. I was once offered his accounting books to buy, but I declined.

The life of a painting is sometimes extraordinary... It was known that Ingres had done three paintings for the Murat family in Naples in 1814, one year before the fall of Napoleon: a portrait of Caroline Murat in mourning in a room in the palace, with a window that looks out over the bay and Vesuvius; the great odalisque, seen from the back, that is in the Louvre and a large odalisque, seen from the front, which has disappeared. The portrait of Caroline Murat had also disappeared. And yet, it was, apparently, with a family in Ravenna who seemed to know nothing of its origins, but who should have known, since their ancestors had served under the Murats in Naples, I later learned. A great critic of Italian art at the time had said that this painting was not by Ingres. Nevertheless, it was bought by Belgian dealers who did some research and found six or eight sketches for the painting in the Montauban Museum. Everything was there: the panorama, the footrest placed sideways, the dress, the hat, etc. It is a work of staggering virtuosity. Incredible stories about paintings almost always exist and those that were believed to be lost always end up being found at some point.

If I love collecting works of art so much, it is because there is nothing that gives me more pleasure than recognizing them. Just as people say: "I recognize my own child", I recognize an object or painting when I buy it. I make it part of my heritage – I know very well that it doesn't really belong to me; it belonged to others before me and will belong to someone else after me – but, for a while, it becomes part of my family, and is a living thing. This is a rather intense phenomenon, which eludes simple logic. Any curator knows full well that a museum only remains vibrant through acquisitions. This is a mystery, but a museum might own great treasures and hold magnificent exhibitions, but if it does not make acquisitions, it ceases to exist because the curator must always have the ability to recognize what is art in the present. The reason my grandfather made no distinction between what he bought for himself and what he bought for museums was that he felt that the work of art had to be acknowledged, whether it was by the Musée Guimet, the Louvre, the Carnavalet or by him, was of no importance. There is a bit of pride in this attitude that consists in the belief that, by making gifts of art, one can make a difference, even in the most beautiful museum collections; there is generosity in this attitude. If you believe that you yourself are privileged, it is normal to help others share in those privileges; and there is respect in this attitude, respect for the superior knowledge of curators; their choices are immediately understandable; we know that they are more legitimate because they are based on knowledge, while our own choices are based only on personal taste. And so there is no more absolute distinction between gifts made to museums and a personal collection. To my grandfather, this was obvious. I feel an affinity to this idea, and that is why I truly enjoy sitting on museum acquisition committees. Deep down, I am almost equally thrilled when I acquire a work of art for myself as when I know it will go to a museum with which I am associated.

At first, desiring a work of art comes as a shock. I do not seek to pounce on it like a predator. I have a very strong desire for it when I acquire it, but then, my relationship with it deepens with every passing day. Therein lies a secret. To me, knowing a work of art intimately, looking at it as if it were the very first day of its creation and seeing it live, is the height of happiness. All affectionate feelings come together. All in all, I do not believe that people love their wives, their mistresses, their children and their works of art in very different ways. And such delight is infinite.

On Being of Jewish Descent

The name David-Weill was invented by my grandfather, David, as was often done amongst members of the bourgeoisie in the 1920s. He added the David, which was his own grandfather's name, so it would sound more refined. In reality, this has rather complicated my life because in hotels, I'm always told: "You have no reservation". But the obvious nature of my name has also spared me a great deal of traditional anti-Semitism. If your name is Dennery, which is a Jewish name in eastern France, people don't know that you are Jewish. When your name is David-Weill, they're not about to launch into anti-Semitic remarks, unless they are extraordinarily stupid!

After the war, in the very chic Saint-Louis school where I was a pupil as my brother Jean had been, no one knew how to pronounce my name. Certain people would say: "de La Ville Vieille". Although I hadn't personally suffered in the lycée in Cannes during the war because I was Jewish, it was in 1945 in Paris, that I encountered a few vicious anti-Semites and one boy in particular who swore at me constantly. One day, I finally went to his house and rang the bell; his father didn't answer the door, but his son stopped insulting me. Years later, I met the father. He was the General Secretary of an insurance company of which I was the Director at the time. He came from a good bourgeois Parisian family, one of whom was even a hero in the Free France movement...

Throughout my entire adulthood, however, I have lived as if the fact of being perceived as Jewish was an advantage. The Socialists didn't dare attack me, even though I was *a priori* a thorn in their side. This was a kind of historical piece of good fortune. It would have been politically incorrect of them to not tip their hat to me, at least slightly, even though I was a horrible Capitalist and therefore a top-ranking enemy. Unfortunately, this advantageous prejudice has now disappeared, or so it seems, because of the pro-Palestinian position of a large part of the French Left in the Middle East conflict.

I come from a strange family since I do not think I have a single ancestor who was not Jewish and simultaneously, it is obvious that my family has not felt very Jewish for quite a long time. My paternal grandmother's family originally came from Portugal. Her ancestors emigrated there from Holland; one of them was an orchestra conductor for William of Orange in England. But on my paternal grandfather's side, the line is linked to eastern France without exception, and has been since the eighteenth century. As for my mother, she came from a mixture of the French, English, Dutch and Belgian educated classes. None of them were religious.

My great grandfather, Alexandre Weill, must have been a theist or an agnostic and both my grandfather and my father lived their lives almost entirely without religion. My maternal grandmother didn't believe in anything; when I asked her why, she answered: "Because my husband did not believe in anything", a reply that I found reactionary, but charming! My mother was an atheist and always had been. The book she kept on her bedside table was *Jean Barois*, by Roger Martin du Gard; it described a young man's discovery of atheism. And the death of her eldest son only served to reinforce her lack of belief. She always used to say: "I do hope, as I believe, that God does not exist; because if he does, I hate him." She was baptised before her first marriage, because she was marrying a Catholic, she told the priest: "Now listen, I am not a believer." "Don't worry," he replied, "You'll get there." But she never got there. My grandfather David David-Weill found his faith during the war but didn't want to be baptised before peace was restored, as he didn't wish to appear to be doing it out of opportunism. And my paternal grandmother only converted to Catholicism after her husband's death, in 1953, because she didn't want to give the impression of following his lead. As for my father, he was baptised at the end of the 1960s. In my opinion, his affairs with women, which were far too numerous to be compatible with his conversion, must have made him hesitate for a long time! But, after his baptism, he became a fiercely devout Catholic.

Whenever I expressed any doubts, he would say: "But it's in the catechism!" It was impossible to have a rational discussion with him.

ON BEING OF JEWISH DESCENT

And yet, my grandfather and my father – in particular my father – whose relationship with the world could be described as somewhat snobbish, only considered that there were two groups of people with whom it was suitable to socialize: the great aristocratic families and important Jewish families. No bitterness, therefore, or desire of any kind to renounce being Jewish. My father liked being surrounding by the Jewish elite of his time. To him, being Jewish meant belonging to an aristocracy. Furthermore, he had ideas that were virtually royalist. He believed that the principal vice of the bourgeoisie was that it had rights but no responsibilities and in this regard, he preferred the system of the *Ancien Régime* because people had responsibilities. My father thought that only the Royalty had retained the right sense of nationalism: on one hand, they very often bore their country's name and on the other – and at the same time – they were distantly related to other royal houses in various countries.

It is the same with the Jews. In New York, you can observe people of Jewish descent from every corner of the world. It is very striking to see the extent to which the German Jews are German, even to the degree that they should be pitied, because they no longer can be German Jews. And that is really a tragedy for them because calling oneself a German Jew after the Shoah is almost impossible. But they are, and it is obvious. You get the same impression with Russian Jews, who are Russian to the core.

Yet, at the same time and without any contradiction, they are related. Though nothing else unites them.

Modern Jewish history is an immense success despite the horrific ordeals they lived through in the twentieth century because of Nazism. All the Jews in certain European countries were eliminated, so much so that visiting Poland, for example, is painful because of this sense of loss which is almost physically unbearable. In spite of all this and right up to today, their success is even more extraordinary because it was created by people who started with absolutely nothing and who were relegated to very subordinate roles for a very long time. In France, they were peddlers, they sold livestock or clothes, or were pawnbrokers because Christians were forbidden to engage in money lending. In addition, for a long time, they were locked into a religion that seemed hardly inclined to a great independence of thought. Judaism is very restrictive: certain foods are forbidden and Jews were obliged to stay in on Shabbat. Such things in no way encourage a social life outside the community. They could not eat with anyone who did not follow the same dietary laws and they couldn't do anything contrary to Jewish principles. In fact, if you apply the precepts of this religion and strictly respect them, you remain very isolated and enclosed within its community, and it was intended that way!

When the French Revolution took place in 1789, it was a hugely important event for all Jews. The thing that has upset me the most in current policies towards the Middle East is that people have not realized, or have not cared, that Jews the world over were pro-French. All of them worshipped the French Revolution because they remembered that the freeing of all their creative energy emanated from the Declaration of the Rights of Man and the fact that France accorded full citizenship to all Jews living in its territory. From January 28, 1790 onwards, the rich merchants from Bayonne and Bordeaux rose to the status of Frenchmen, as did the Jews of Alsace-Lorraine on September 27, 1791. Unfortunately, this love of France no longer exists, which makes me extremely sad: France provided a wealth of love and good will that was unique.

There is no doubt at all that in the twentieth century, the liberation of the Jewish community produced a sort of explosion in every possible and imaginable direction: scientific, literary, financial, cinematographic... Moreover, this explosion is one of the essential components of the modern age because the Jews are a mainspring for change, which is irritating. One could write a history of anti-Semitism from the perspective of the need and the desire to advance, or the revulsion and fear such advancement evokes. Every time people are against change, they want to lock up the Jews; every time change seems desirable, the Jews advance. Between the two wars, they represented change, while society as a whole turned back to traditional values. Now, whatever is a return to the past is detrimental to the Jews by definition. On the other hand, everything that represents change – I won't call it progress, as I don't believe in that – suits them.

Today, we are witnessing a true revival of anti-Semitism in France; I mean a rejection of Jews because they are Jewish. It might be re-emerging with different eccentricities but deep down, it is always the same: there is only one anti-Semitism. Either the Jews are accused of being the medium for revolution or the lackeys of Capitalism - and sometimes the two both at once. If this feeling is revived, the form it takes matters little. The position of the Jewish community, as a whole, is in favor of Israel and this is at odds with current European opinion. Moreover, it means that the Jewish community tends to be closer to the United States. These are principal factors in this revival of anti-Semitism. The second element, which is currently the most fearsome, springs from the attitude of a great number of Muslim immigrants who consider Jews their natural enemy, while the question of integration should bring them closer to the Jews. In addition, a large part of public opinion is tired of hearing about the massacre of the Jews during the Second World War. Many other atrocities have happened since then and people have had enough of being reminded, sixty years later, about the genocide of the Jews. The commemoration of the liberation of the death camps in 2005 was inevitable and, in my opinion, harmful, in the sense that this incessant reminder ends up antagonizing people for the wrong reasons. I too participated in it, since I contributed to the construction of the Jewish Memorial in the Marais district in Paris. However, sixty years on, people prefer to become indignant over more recent crimes in Asia or Africa. What is more, the genocide of the Jews constitutes a European crime, which arouses shame, guilt and, consequently, resentment.

Any event that leads to the rejection of one group of the population seriously damages national unity. If the French style of integration has its virtues where the Jewish question is concerned, it might also bring with it – to top it all off – a jealous reaction about how their misfortune is regarded. Others believe that they too have suffered and that nothing is being done for them... Unemployment affects them the most, they cannot obtain decent housing, they have to prove they are more able than others, etc. We do not have enough examples of success coming from the poor suburbs. The Right wing has recently made an effort, but this effort is still in its infancy compared to what is being done in the United States. The French Left believed that by denying the problem for more than twenty years, it would go away. This is not only a lie, it is an error whose negative effects can be seen more and more with the passage of time. In addition, becoming a French citizen should be something to be proud of, but that assumes that the French themselves are proud of it...

My father did not approve of the creation of the State of Israel. He saw it as the beginning of new problems. My attitude is different: I have friends who are in a difficult situation in the Middle East and if I can help them, I am happy to. Therefore, much to the surprise of the Jewish community in France or America, I have always been loyal to Jewish charities. I do not see why you can't have various strata in your identity: rather than contradicting one another, they complement each other. I have never avoided the subject of Jewishness, but I haven't broached it either, not even with my children. I didn't tell them: "You know, we're Jewish" or: "You know, we're not Jewish". My children do not see this as a problem in either sense. They suffered anti-Semitic remarks when they were young, but that can't be avoided in childhood. They seem to me very comfortable with their double or triple personality, and I believe that like me, they are happier for it.

Not only am I glad to be of Jewish descent or, as Sartre would put it, to be "a Jewish atheist", but I feel very influenced by belonging to a Jewish family from eastern France. This fact is bound up with my sense of nationalism and even reinforces it. My ancestors considered themselves French above all else and were very patriotic. When Germany seized Alsace-Lorraine from France in 1870, the event greatly contributed to the development of this patriotism, which was actually rather pro the Republic, and the effect was very powerful in the Jewish communities in eastern France. My father's family comes from Phalsbourg, a military city in Lorraine, founded under Louis XIV. It is a rather beautiful city, laid out on a grid, with two great gates, the *Porte de France* and the *Porte d'Allemagne*. As in many cities in Alsace-Lorraine, there is a street where the Jews lived next to the cathedral. It is named after my great grandfather, Alexandre Weill: the house where he was born is next to the synagogue. His own father was also born in Phalsbourg, in 1790. Consequently, and strangely or not, I cannot imagine myself as completely French without recalling my Jewish roots in eastern France.

Books by Erckmann-Chatrian, which no one ever reads anymore and whose idealized goodness I adore, describe the society of these small towns in Alsace-Lorraine very well. Added to this, Erckmann was my grandfather's teacher at the Lycée Condorcet. *Le Blocus* tells the story of a Jewish family from Phalsbourg and, in *L'Ami Fritz* which takes place on the other side of the Rhine, I am told that the character of the Rabbi was based on my great grandfather's uncle, and there is proof that this is true.

When the Vichy government stripped my grandfather of his French citizenship on the pretext that he had gone abroad in 1940, even though he came back a few weeks later saying that he wanted to die in France, it was a terrible experience for him. Even more so since one has to remember that at the time no distinction was made between Vichy and France. The difference only emerged later and, consequently, the shock was even more brutal then... He did, however, regain his citizenship during the war, during the Riom trial, because they had to accept the evidence that he had not wanted to leave his country. Nevertheless, robbing him of his citizenship had wounded him to the very core. I have always retained this sense of patriotism, which is very much alive in my family. And I, who do not have very revolutionary tendencies and do not even believe in the virtue of revolutions, even I cannot forget that it was the French Revolution, before the Terror came to ruin everything, that made it possible for the Jews of France to be granted citizenship, something that Louis XVI had earlier desired.

In New York, where there are two million Jews out of a population of eight million inhabitants, their influence is considerable. If you have the feeling that the entire city is Catholic on Ash Wednesday because all the Catholics have ashes on their foreheads, on Yom Kippur, you truly have the impression of being in a city that is entirely Jewish. New York is deserted, there is no traffic, offices on Wall Street are half empty... It is probable that this Jewish population includes rather fewer unintelligent people than average, but also a number at least equal, if not greater, of idiots! I believe that intelligence can lead people to do stupid things, and that is what I call idiocy. There are many idiots in the Jewish population in general, but there are not many unintelligent people. In other populations, there are more unintelligent people than idiots, which isn't much better, when all is said and done, but it does make a difference. What I mean by unintelligent is someone who lacks intelligence, while an idiot is a person who is illogical. I think that the fact of being on average more intelligent – even if there are many idiots – comes from Holy Scripture, that is to say, from reading the Bible, from pursuing an intellectual activity and therefore being able to constantly question oneself. At the French Lycée in New York where I was a student when I was a teenager, one of our teachers, Mr. Tricot (son of the General Secretary of the Élysée Palace when General de Gaulle was President and who was rather a left-wing Christian himself) had finally understood that we were all unconsciously being influenced by the Talmud when he saw that instead of answering his questions, we asked other questions! The Jews learned to read the Bible and contradict it; this brings with it an entire process of questioning, quibbling, an intellectual propensity to understand and grasp other people's points of view and a constant quest for something new: all these qualities are specifically recognizable traits in the Jewish community.

In my opinion, what distinguishes different peoples in the world is whether or not they have a thirst for education. The Jews prosper in times when inventions are needed; they do not prosper when innovation is rejected. The Jews have both a tradition and a thirst for education. They believe that knowledge is quasi-sacred. All the Jewish jokes about "my son the doctor" reveal how important this is.

ON BEING OF JEWISH DESCENT

There is a wonderful tradition and an extraordinary variety of talents among Jews throughout the world. When I was going to Brazil, I discovered that one of my mother's first cousins was a Brazilian national hero. His name was Pierre Verger and he was a photographer and ethnologist. Today, in Salvador, the capital of Bahia, he is considered the holy of all holies in a religion that originated in Africa, called *candomblé*. He first lived in Dahomey where he became very interested in the religion, customs and medicines of Yarouba. He even wrote a very scholarly dictionary on the subject. He then revived the *candomblé* religion in Brazil. When I visited there, if I said I was the cousin of Pierre Verger, even in very sophisticated social circles or at formal dinners, people would swoon with delight. Here was someone who had been completely rejected by his family, who had led the life of a poor man in Brazil and who became a national hero in an esoteric field. How that reveals his amazing journey, destiny, intellectual curiosity and independence of spirit!

What makes the Jews dear to my heart is their sense of humor, which I share, and their anxiety, which means that the Jewish people you meet are rarely confident about their rightful place in society. Their anxiety is born of their sense of having been uprooted and the fact that, quite correctly, they can never be sure what tomorrow might bring. This is also an element in my personality; it means that while I do not expect the worst to happen, I am never surprised when it does. It is normal when things go wrong, normal that people don't like you or stop liking you and reject you for one reason or another... This way of seeing life is not individual: it must be genetic.

In any case, my Jewish origins certainly play a role. I truly understand their psychology, which facilitated my relationships with people on Wall Street, where there are many Jews today. This was not always the case because there was a time, and not very long ago, when they were not allowed to work there. Nevertheless, I feel out of step with them: I do not know their religion any more than I know Islam and I only experience their traditions as an outsider. So I have given up my right to be Jewish, but I do understand them.

I have a romantic view of the human saga of the Jews and even if I do not consider myself truly one of them, I still feel great sympathy toward them, sometimes mixed in with annoyance at the idea that nothing is ever simple for them. I will only add that it is rather funny that the only person in my family who has Israeli citizenship is named Gérard de La Fressange. He is the grandson of André Lazard and has spent his entire life working as a docker in Haifa, because he chose to represent Christ as a Catholic priest of the Order of the Brothers of Foucault in this non-Christian environment.

On the Church

"You are French" my father said to me one day, "I believe it is more sensible to take the religion of the majority of Frenchmen." And that was all he said. And so it happened that I was taken in hand by one of my aunts, Simone Lazard (who had married Maurice Petsch, Minister of Finance after the war, one of the only representatives who, although he was right-wing, still voted against Pétain.) I can remember my Baptism perfectly… It was in Briançon in 1941; I was eight years old. The church was damp, my aunt delighted, and, as for me, I was slightly surprised to find myself there.

As an adolescent in New York after the war, I became a practicing Catholic. I went to Mass more than once a week at the Jesuit church, St. Ignatius Loyola, in the neighborhood where I lived; and later on, as a university student at the School of Political Science in Paris, I regularly went to the Jesuit center on the Rue de la Chaise. Nevertheless, no one in my family talked about religion. But during my teenage years in New York, as always happened in my life, I met a very kind priest. He was called

Father Farine and he became one of my guiding lights. I still remember going for a walk with him when he turned towards me and exclaimed: "Michel, I don't think I have ever met anyone who will be sent to Hell." "You are undoubtedly right" I heard myself say, like an idiot who responds glibly to a deep idea, before realising how very remarkable it was to hold such a belief. It demonstrated so much generosity of spirit…

All my life, I have enjoyed meeting clergymen. One of my friends, Philippe Ader, with whom I went on a long trip to the Far East with my sister during the mid-1950s, even found religion there, based entirely on the example of Father de Foucauld. We were twenty years old. In the evening, we would leave my sister at the hotel and go out to all the local dives. We knew virtually every inch of them! When we got to Japan, after travelling through Iran, India, Indochina and Thailand, I could see that, as our journey progressed, my friend showed less enthusiasm for such things, but I told myself he was probably just tired. In fact, he had already found faith during our stay in Thailand. He hadn't said anything to me but he had confided in my sister. Once back in France, I saw him often, because, like me, he was called back into the army during what came to be known as the Bizerte uprisings in Tunisia, and he no longer read anything except theology books.

His father had been afraid that this expedition to the other side of the world with a spoiled, wealthy young man like me might prevent him from seeing the realities of life, especially since I have never hesitated to travel in the most luxurious style possible, and yet this is where he found God. What's more, he went back to live in Pakistan, which we had visited, and spent his entire life as a worker in the order of the Order of the Brothers of Foucauld, founded by Charles de Foucauld.

A few years later, I saw him again at my office in Paris, and, not so long ago, he came and had lunch with me in my house in the Midi. As he was a friend, when I saw him again, I was able to ask him some questions that, in general, one wouldn't ask a priest. I asked him whether he missed women a lot, and he replied: "Less than I miss cars!" It's true that he used to love driving really beautiful fast cars…

In Rome, in the Holy Year of 1950, my Catholic faith reached its summit. Piously, I went to Mass and took communion in each one of the basilicas, as we were expected to do. I am a solitary soul, yet I enjoyed participating in the community of the Church, along with Christians from all over the world who walked in processions down the streets, fervently chanting the same canticles. What always pleased me about Catholicism, was its rites, and I rather miss Latin because the Liturgy in that language was so captivating that it incarnated the faith in a very convincing manner.

And then, while still continuing to love the Church and support Catholic charities, I lost my faith. I sincerely believe that man is a species of animal like any other and that there are only minor differences between the species. Deep down, I am wary of man's pretension in believing himself so superior to other animals that he invents a God unique to our species, and I am wary of the impertinence of Christianity in particular which not only embraces this idea, but maintains in addition that God became incarnate in man, an idea which seems to me unbelievably arrogant! This would mean thinking that we, as human beings, are at the center of the universe, something I no longer believe. The universe is vast, our planet occupies but a small part of it, and even if we are endowed with the gift of speech and a greater capacity for reasoning, our instincts, on the whole, are not so very different from those of other species. The origins of all religions seem unhealthy, because they are founded, or so it appears to me, on the impossibility of accepting our status as an animal. I absolutely do not believe that we are so important and so different from dogs, cats and horses, to the extent that there is someone up above who watches over us. We are animals who, through chance good fortune, have mildly improved ourselves in relation to other animals, though not much, and we have no reason to take pride in this. Rather, we have more defects than almost any other species of animal, and, in particular the insatiable thirst for killing which is virtually unique to human beings. There are only chimpanzees, who are so close to us genetically, who kill for the sake of killing. The majority of other animals kill for food and, in any case, it is only man who wages war. It is therefore logical, to my mind, that there is nothing terribly special in store for us in another world, and it seems to be quite simply unreasonable to imagine a possible link between the human and the supernatural.

Despite all this, it would never occur to me to carry out any sort of campaign about it. Not out of a concern for conventions… I simply don't see the need. I am not a believer, but of what importance is that! If one believes in God, it is very important, but if one does not believe, it changes nothing if others do… And besides, I am moved by the humility of believers who feel themselves dependent on something greater than themselves, and I dislike the relatively wide-spread notion that there is a correlation between not believing in God and the idea of thinking oneself to be superior. I would be happy to think that someone believed himself to be an animal, but I would not like to think that someone believed himself a God!

Nor have I ever understood how belief in the hereafter might bring any sort of comfort. If I believed in that, it would be a source of the greatest concern… It is not pleasant to have to be judged. Not believing in the hereafter seems very reassuring to me. But I have always thought that the Church, thanks to this belief, prepares people to die with charity. And, consequently, I have always helped Catholic institutions who tend the sick.

If we owe a debt of gratitude to Pope John Paul II, it is because he validated illness and death through the example of his own end. In the present day, we hide people who are dying, we're ashamed of them, and we virtually believe that if someone falls ill, it's his own fault. He drank too much or smoked too much, so he's being punished. Death is concealed; the dying are taken to hospital and their bodies disappear. But the Pope had the courage to show how he suffered, how he fought and how he lost. When he tried to speak during his final public appearance at Easter, he couldn't manage to and he didn't hide it: it was absolutely wonderful. Everyone protested: "This Pope must resign, he should disappear, we mustn't see him die!" He came to terms with his death, and so did us a great service. Vulnerability exists, it was visible, it concerns each and every one of us without exception, and there is no point in denying it. I have a deep admiration for him. It was so clear that his faith was real, it was so obvious, as with his successor Benedict XVI, that this fact creates something eminently respectable, something we call humility. When you are the head of a government, you are expected to have an air of importance. Now the Pope *is* important, but he doesn't think he is.

I had the opportunity of meeting John Paul II in Rome, when he granted an audience to members of the Trilateral Commission, the international organization to which I belong and where political, cultural and especially economic matters are debated. Well, he gave us all quite a telling off … making an anti-capitalist speech that could do nothing but displease me!

The Catholic Church admires and respects poverty, which is a beautiful and necessary concept. But a certain perversion has crept into this idea: that is, making poverty a virtue, an idea that exists in the Gospels. As a result, and from the very beginning, a great deal of mistrust was established with regard to economic development. To lift people out of poverty actually represents the risk that they might become materialistic, and the rich even more so, since they have possessions. This anxiety at seeing people concerned with increasing their own wealth therefore remains at the heart of the Church's concerns. The Christian ideal is the monastery: everyone is equally poor, and, through their poverty they are free to dedicate themselves to serving God. Everything else is a waste of time and involves the risk of going to Hell. Looking after the poor, lifting people's spirits, giving them spirituality and discipline in life are all fine ideals, but, where economics are concerned, the Church is a nuisance! Clergymen are perhaps right; I have infinite respect for them and I am not saying they should change their opinions. Nevertheless, while it is not against the religion of Protestants and Jews to attempt to elevate themselves to a better economic state, it is utterly contradictory in Catholicism.

However, to me, the idea of pardon is a magnificent Catholic invention. Instead of a world of implacable justice, there exists a universe of clemency where anyone may redeem himself. It is a lofty idea, perhaps the most beautiful of all, and one I consider very real and very valuable. If one considers the values of Christianity as a whole, then having refused to include the idea that Europe embodies a Christian tradition in the European Constitution seems incomprehensible to me. All you have to do is go for a walk in any village and you will see that many are named after Saints and that a church steeple is never far away... Of course, other religions and cultures have made valuable contributions, but Christianity is at the heart of who we are. To deny this is therefore to renounce what gives us our identity as Europeans.

Today, my strongest link with Catholicism is actually an aesthetic one. I am deeply indebted to the Church for the way it has created respect for each man as a unique individual and for having adopted beauty as one of its moral values, something which, to my mind, is admirable. And of course, Western Art owes everything to Christianity. How could we ever forget that?

On Women

I love women because of their shape, their skin, their charm, their beauty, and I also believe they possess an abundance of humanity that they find difficult to forget. I have always had the vague suspicion that women were the only truly human beings, which is why I find them superior to men. Perhaps this is an illusion, but it does seem to me that deep within every woman is a person who does not think in clichés. For a woman, nothing is ever set in stone. Freedom is always possible and there are no pre-established truths: their opinions, desires, tastes can change and evolve from one moment to the next. This way of approaching life might be hidden behind as many social facades as you like, but it is still there. Men, on the other hand, retain a great faculty for forgetting their human side; they create personas for themselves instead. I recognize one virtue in men and only one: energy. What is attractive about men is a certain delight they take in action, an urge that is often stronger than in women. This is probably because men are free of certain physical constraints linked to very early childhood and child bearing, so they can more easily exhibit their instinct to act. But I find that women get along better in life; they have fewer artificial hurdles when dealing with their doubts and are more dependable and less inclined to talk nonsense. Curiously, however, men who truly like women are rare. In general, they prefer to play soccer or socialize with other men... Since I don't play sports, I've had more time.

I have always had very strong relationships with the women in my life, whether it was with my wife, Hélène, or my daughters, Béatrice, Cécile, Natalie and Agathe. I am very close to them because I love them just as they are. It is the same with my sister Éliane whose affection has been very precious to me since my childhood and greatly adds to my happiness. My grandmothers also played an important role in my life; I even lived with my maternal grandmother while I was a student at Sciences-Po. She was an adorable woman, very cheerful, whom I encouraged to learn Chinese. I enjoy the same strong relationships with my closest women friends and, of course, with my mother: she was such an important influence and was the model for my concept of women.

My mother was extremely independent, with extraordinary strength and presence. She shaped her own identity after her divorce and conquered Parisian high society between the two world wars. She was emancipated, very in control, intellectual and passionate. Add to that immense courage and authority and a kind of will of steel in a tiny body, what I might call an ironclad but delicate constitution. She was born Berthe Haardt and came from a middle-class Jewish family from Brussels. They fled Belgium in 1914 when the Germans occupied the country and never went back. Her grandfather was a diamond merchant of Dutch descent; her father had built the tramways in Odessa and one of her relatives, Georges-Marie Haardt, had led the *Croisière noire et jaune*, (the famous Citroën international car rallies) in Africa and Asia during the 1920s. She spoke to me as an adult even when I was a child, asking my advice very early on, which I found quite normal. At the age of seven, I was the center of the universe! She loved me and I loved her. She always had a unique way of making our conversations special. She would arrange for just the two of us to have breakfast together so we could talk; she called it a picnic. And I have begun the same ritual with my daughters: whenever they are in Paris, they take it in turn to come and have breakfast with me. Like my mother, I really only believe in one-to-one conversations; this is how I feel true exchanges take place. Everything else is nothing more than pretence and doesn't really work, except on exceptional family occasions, sometimes happy ones, sometimes tragic.

In 1946, I began attending the Lycée français in New York, which was already co-educational. For the first time in my life, I found myself surrounded by girls, and I got on wonderfully well with the female third of the class. My best friends were girls even back then, and always have been throughout my life. One of them, whom I liked very much, was the daughter of one of the former governors of the French colonies; another was a charming American, and yet another was always first in the class. They were extremely kind to me: if I hadn't done my homework in the morning, they would help me. All in all, it was very pleasant. I was interested to know what they thought, I liked having them around and I was in no way predatory.

I basically had the mentality of a modern man in 1950: I was a feminist before its time.

All of that was wonderful but with one disadvantage: it eliminated the powerfully masculine side of me when it came to chasing women. Having so much consideration for your mother, sister and female relatives means that you do not look at women as prey. It was so engrained in me to respect women, however unintentionally, that I could never comprehend the idea of claiming a woman rather than asking for her. And this is surely not normal, or so I concluded fifty years later! It was as if I had virtually lost a genetically transmitted instinct... And my father impressed me unbelievably by his total confidence where women were concerned! I have never seen anything like it because it was completely natural, which was obviously very upsetting to his wife... If he liked a woman and by a stroke of luck she also liked him, he never imagined there could be the least obstacle; it never even occurred to him! And because he was so very at ease, he won their favors. They would say: "Well, why not?" It was totally extraordinary! Such incredible freedom...

We really must face the facts: women do not dislike predators. Even since a female friend taught me to like animals, I have noticed that being a predator is natural, but it is not in my nature. In many groups of monkeys, the dominant male is not always by definition the strongest. As a general rule, however, the most predatory prevail when it comes to reproduction. Now, we have masked our animalistic behavior by dressing it up in fine feelings and lofty ideas. It remains nevertheless true that this animalistic factor is central to our attitudes and is evident everywhere, in the business world and in personal relationships.

These days, our society is becoming more feminized. This is why many people today believe that anything is better than war, an idea primarily held by the majority of women. Certain women in the past, of course, have fought heroically and could do so again, but most of them still think that that nothing is worth either killing for or dying for. This is a heavenly kind of pacifism but is also somewhat suicidal because if you lay your cards on the table by announcing: "I won't defend myself", this very fact becomes a genuine incentive to crime. On another level, playing with taboos while not actually defying them by surfing the Net looking for sexual encounters which remain virtual, seems to me to stem from an attitude that is more typical of the female psyche than the male. It is a new kind of sophisticated banter that you can participate in without getting hurt too much. And even if boys did what they always did thirty years ago, that is, chased women, young women also chased men. Today, young people couple off very quickly, and the boys who are sweet, cute, kind and intelligent are the ones who are successful with girls, while a virile boy finds himself marginalized – proof that feminine attitudes have won out here, as elsewhere. We are therefore in the process of transforming the species by means of sexual attraction.

Yet more and more women are complaining of the lack of men. People like each other because of their differences, but we act as if we are alike and then… we drop them. Professionally, there is the opposite tendency. Any woman can succeed as long as she acts like a man. She must have masculine instincts to survive; she must change her behavior and adapt to the pace devised by and for men. In other words, she must be manly. I am reminded of something that Guillaume Apollinaire said about "the eternal differences between men and women". I think it is a question of being necessarily complementary. To call a woman "feminine" is to picture her as a curious mixture of the essential and the superfluous. Men rarely have in mind what is fundamental, while women think more about life, birth, the long-term. And at the same time, they pay attention to the little details of life that make it more agreeable, something that men rarely do. It might be paradoxical to say that men care more about appearances, but I think it is true. Women are stylish, but this is just their way of making life more beautiful and it is not essential. Deep down, women know what is really important. Men don't.

Oscillating between these two extremes does have a disadvantage: concentrating on a career becomes less straightforward. To find a solution, too many women have chosen the masculine camp. This is a disaster... There is another way, and that is to adopt a type of thinking that is more complex than the way most men think. Women often display more selflessness at work while simultaneously refusing to forget what is central to life. Men find this thought process rather disconcerting because it oscillates between enthusiasm and an urge to go back to what is essential. Because such behavior is more complex, it leads to a degree of erratic behaviour that is in contradiction to the simplistic binary understanding of situations by men.

Another paradox is that Western man has become the role model for the entire world, not Western woman. The

Chinese found it very easy to become Westernized, as did the Indians, to such an extent that there are fake Western men everywhere now. And it is a veritable triumph! With a bit of distance, they have managed to surpass the original model, as it is not very difficult to play at being a Western man; moreover, this is the key to their success. It would be infinitely more complicated to pretend to be Mandarin! How do we recognize Western man? He displays a lack of interest in metaphysics, has simple aspirations and is materialistic. His relationships with others are kept to a minimum and a weakening social structure. In the past, events and ideas had a meaning that one had to know and understand. Today, people everywhere are all alike.

Life is much easier to live practically. Everyone knows what he wants: he wants more, not what's better. And it's the same everywhere.

When I was young, I found myself in rather an awkward position where women were concerned, which was not very helpful when it came to seducing them. But I was loved a great deal and ultra-modern in my attitude towards women. When I met Hélène, my future wife, she was a very shy, reserved young woman who kept herself to herself. I found this very appealing because I could sense that behind all her defences was an enormous amount of love that she wasn't expressing. I enjoy telling the story of the first time I saw her: it was on the Champs-Élysées and I was eighteen years old. I was going to the movies and she was walking along with a girlfriend whom I also knew. Hélène comes from the only Catholic banking family in France, the Lehideux. One of her uncles had been a Minister under the Vichy government, but her relatives had fallen out with him. Her grandfather held the post of President of the *Association française des banques*; he had the reputation of being very anti-Semitic, and I believe it was true. Hélène's mother came from an aristocratic family from Franche-Comté who owned the very beautiful Château de Moncley near Besançon, which everyone loved. Our marriage posed no problem at all in my family, but in hers, it was more complicated... I was unaware of all it at the time, but I probably would not have been able to marry Hélène if I hadn't been Catholic.

It was during those early years that Hélène developed a rather strong personality, as she wished to be independent and make her own choices. She defied a certain number of social conventions by ignoring them, which made her a rather unique and very attractive young woman. Because of this, she didn't worry at all about what her family might think if she ended up marrying me, but she must have shown great determination in order to do so. Her parents were more worried, however, than negative about it. "Those people aren't like us," they thought, "It will be complicated..." We finally were married in the Midi, at the Church of Sainte-Hélène de La Garoupe, in July 1956. I was twenty-three years old; I wanted children and longed to truly start living.

Just like works of art, my children add to my *joie de vivre*. I have enjoyed having them a great deal, and to feel their abundant physical presence – four enchanting little souls, since they were all girls – has always delighted me. Their imagination was very appealing. One day, I taught one of them how to beat her wings so she could fly away. Her mother became rather worried and asked her if she really thought she could fly. "Of course not!" she replied. What is wonderful about children is that they can be fanciful while still remaining logical... Hélène would certainly have loved to have a boy, both for herself and for me. But I am rather philosophical on the subject, since having a son would not have guaranteed he would one day be an heir who was capable of taking over Lazard... One of my daughters might have expressed a desire to succeed me, but none of them ever did... They aren't fools!

It would have been necessary to put the business before everything else. None of them wanted to do that, and it would never occur to me to hold that against them.

Are they like their mother or like me? My daughters are unique individuals and since I always live in the present, I never notice any resemblance that reminds me of the past. We share almost everything, with a similar view of the world, and that is why they have the distinctive characteristic of belonging to my family. They have seen the same things, gained experience of life that brings them closer to mine: they are not strangers to the world of art, or to the United States, or to France. I feel I am unique, but not unique where they are concerned because they share my way of seeing life. I have often been rather difficult because I have always believed that children should learn responsibility from quite an early age. There are very few things I cannot tolerate. Actually, there is only one: rudeness. I find it unbearable not to be considerate when speaking to someone. I have never been strict with my daughters, never lectured them or tried to teach them lessons. Everything was learned by osmosis and by example. I wanted them to have good manners and they do! They make an effort and are not vain. They are people whom I would be pleased to meet even if I didn't know them. The fact remains, however, that I sometimes find my wife's independent spirit even more entertaining. When a couple knows each other since their youth, which is our case, each influences how the other develops. The beginning of our marriage was quite volatile, because I was very possessive, jealous, and because I imposed my old habits. And then, with time, when the other person's reactions are not what you expect, you come to understand them, accept them, enjoy them. It is a long journey... Hélène has some cut and dried opinions and is sometimes vehement, but never with me. She has made my life beautiful; she knows how to organize our life wonderfully, how to surround herself with just the right people and she is very French, which is one of her charms.

People have often asked me: "What is the greatest virtue of the French?" I invariably reply: the relationships between French men and women. They are unique in the world: respect, affection, deference, no contempt, a true liking of others, genuine understanding, whereas the English and Americans live in very separate worlds: the paths of men and women do not cross because each group has its own preoccupations. In France, it is easy to speak to a woman from the outset, but the art of sidestepping issues inherent in any sophisticated conversation makes it difficult to get to know the real person. In New York, on the other hand, since the art of sociability is less refined, you immediately find yourself face to face with the real woman. A French woman is essentially a person, and you understand her as such, while in the United States, people define themselves first and foremost by their profession or circumstances. This is just as true for men as for women. And yet, the protective bubble in which each individual encloses himself is more resilient in France than in the United States. It is therefore easier to get close to an American woman than to a Frenchwoman: once the social barrier has been crossed, you can understand them more directly. But politeness is so engrained in France that any attempt at closeness takes a very long time. While it might be easier to have a pleasant conversation with a Frenchwoman, the outstanding qualities of American women can be revealed because there are fewer social taboos. They have not been schooled in the art of conversation but rather tend to reflect the openness of the American character, which is so closely linked to the sense of space of this great country. This type of encounter makes it possible to better comprehend America and leads to a different type of understanding of nature and the world.

Living Between America and France

I have the great joy of living between two countries, the United States and France, which gives me the opportunity of savoring contrasting delights. The pleasure of American democracy comes from its dynamism, though this makes a certain type of elegance difficult. It also makes the idea of the future dangerous because everything changes so quickly and because you have to be ready for battle while continually adapting in order to survive. The pleasure of living in French society derives from a taste for refinement that is much more pronounced in the privileged classes and which leads a large part of the population to hate those who symbolize this way of life. As a result, the atmosphere in France is not always pleasant, but life there can be agreeable. It has a feeling of camaraderie based on communal tastes that does not exist across the Atlantic. On the other hand, there are friendly relations in the United States based more on similar aspirations, and being committed to the same journey creates a community.

A TASTE FOR HAPPINESS

When I first went to New York in 1946, the city was already an unbelievable spectacle of life, opulence, color and movement that gave me the impression of immense blossoming, optimism and cheerfulness. Before buying one of those wonderful houses on Fifth Avenue that still existed at the time, my father owned an apartment on Central Park South. It wasn't very big. My bed was set up in the dining room; it looked out onto Broadway and was all lit up at night. And, from the other side of the apartment, I never tired of watching the red and yellow taxis pass by in the streets and the park... It was a dazzling sight! At the time, I didn't speak English very well. The first time I took a bus, I realized that I didn't know how much it cost or how to ask. I was left very much to my own devices. My parents were wonderful but, unlike today, it didn't occur to them to spend much time with their children. I did see them of course; I'm not saying that I never ate dinner with them, but it was only about two or three times a week. If they went to the country for the weekend, they wouldn't dream of taking us with them. Later on, thanks to my wife Hélène, I learned that people did such things; I would not have thought of it myself.

At the Lycée Français in New York, I found myself in a social circle that was very different from the ones I'd been used to until then. For the first time in my life, I had friends who included a boy whose father had been a Spanish Republican General and whose mother was a Russian Communist, a girl from central Europe who was very pro-Zionist, several sons of local French chefs, the sons of diplomats... Every trimester, the pupils voted for a class representative. I was in the fourth year and on the day of the election, the boy sitting next to me said: "You'll win, you'll see." No one had said anything to me about it. "Surely not," I replied, "Why would I?" And I got elected. You couldn't hold the post for two trimesters in a row, but I was voted in every other time. It was rather inexplicable because I never sought the honor. But being elected did me a lot of good, even though I didn't consider it an extraordinary accomplishment. Given my ability to contain and isolate anything I find disagreeable, I do not therefore get overly excited by what is pleasant. But I realized that I could be relatively popular and that secretly made me happy.

In New York, I always organized my life with a certain delight at being independent, free, and foreign – that is to say, with no responsibilities. The joy of being a foreigner is first and foremost feeling you are not accountable: whatever displeases you does not affect you. Having no commitments is delightful! In France, I often take opinions, feelings and prevailing prejudices too much to heart and I am upset by the excitement or anger of my countrymen. For example, I recall having been against the Algerian War from the very beginning and unhappy to feel I was opposed to the majority of the French. I never had any doubts on the subject, but it doesn't help much to be right... I was also against the war in Vietnam, while people I knew in New York were for it, but that in no way bothered me. Moreover, given my spirit of contradiction, by the end of the conflict, I had come to feel that the Americans shouldn't pull out, and found myself being shouted at by the very people who had told off me when I was against the war!

With hindsight, I consider it an unbelievable privilege to have been able to participate in life in the United States: its dynamism is at the heart of the world and I have always felt myself very fortunate to witness it. Being a foreigner never counted against me or against the Lazard Bank because there is no xenophobia whatsoever in the business world in the United States. On the other hand, it is impossible to imagine how difficult it is to relate to people on a day-to-day basis when you do not share their culture. I do not know the rules of baseball; I have never attended a football match. Now, Americans are passionate about sports, to such an extent that it is one of their most popular topics of conversation. So it is better to like a sport, any sport, because this makes socializing and conversation easier. Yet I never could manage it. When I told an American lady friend of mine that I didn't know anyone at the golf club where I have happily been a member for more than twenty years, she understood me perfectly but replied that she wasn't sure I should brag about it! The fact that I was not truly part of American society has not really concerned me too much. On the other hand, when I briefly was the head of Lazard London, in 1984, I realized that it would be even more difficult to become integrated into British society because I would have to take part in social activities. I had neither the time nor probably the ability to do so, for it is much more difficult to be English than American!

Only two countries in the world believe they have a universal mission: the United States and France. You are not English simply by declaring you are English or if you speak English, but you are American if you declare yourself American, and French if you speak French. This is the reason why these two countries are constantly at odds with each other. Two close yet different views of the world do battle to conquer people's spirits. Nothing like this happens in England. You might be accepted but you will never really be in the inner circle, with very rare exceptions. I had the good fortune of amusing the English because being an iconoclast is better accepted in England than in France or the United States. When you say something that goes against current ideas, the English find it entertaining. While that kind of things makes the French and the Americans furious, the English have a kind of tradition of eccentricity. And so I feel rather at home in England, thanks to the impression that I enjoy great freedom there because there are fewer taboo subjects than anywhere else. Try saying in France: "Why don't we do an experiment and get rid of income tax? Let's give it a try on a regional level, in any region, and see if that area has better economic growth than another." People would respond: "How would we pay for Social Security? Change? – Impossible!" I wouldn't say it; I wouldn't even dare think it. In England, people would say: "He's unique. He may be wrong, but he has his own opinion." In the United States, were you dare to suggest: "I think we should get rid of the army," the Americans would go mad! Or in France, "I don't see any problem if the Muslims want to wear the veil." In England, many Muslims do wear it, and it is of no importance whatsoever.

But perhaps that is changing...

The French do not want to acknowledge any differences between them. There is a famous joke that everyone has learned: "Our ancestors, the Gauls..."

Consequently, they refuse to allow anyone to state they are French but different because they were born in Algeria, China, Africa, etc. The Jewish community was forced to call themselves French and feel themselves to be French while not being able to show any outward signs of being Jewish; it is considered very bad taste to wear religious symbols, even a hat. Public opinion in France considers that, to be French, you have to have external signs that confirm you as French, which is not at all the case in the United States. And French society does not seem ready to change on this point, not ready to accept that you can be French while simultaneously expressing true loyalty to something else. This is not generally accepted. I disagree and do not see why people shouldn't display signs of their faith, though I would not go as far as to ally myself with people who want to destroy the world in which I live. Since there is a battle between those who say: "We claim our right as Muslims to deal with problems according to Sharia law", and others who state: "We claim our right as Frenchmen to preserve our full national identity", you must choose a side. Because unfortunately, if you don't choose, you find yourself on the other side.

As Winston Churchill is claimed to have said: "Do you want to vote with your opinions as a hooligan or with your party as a gentleman?" Up to a certain point, the idea of secularity in France is rather beautiful and inspirational, insofar as being a French citizen takes precedence over everything else and is the incentive for equality among all men. But what was once the virtue of French-style integration is currently preventing it.

The United States taught their black population to be proud of being black, their Hispanics proud to be Hispanic, in return for which today, they are all Americans. Integration was encouraged in a wonderful way, by allowing people to display their foreign characteristics. And as a result, everyone feels they belong to the country in which they live. By rejecting different national characteristics, France has partially failed in its system of integration. Moreover, French society is composed of well-defined social classes, which is not the case in American society.

I am one of those people who love everything that has been handed down, more or less, from the enlightened attitude of the eighteenth century French aristocracy: a certain kind of courtesy, way of behaving, selflessness, loftiness of thought, refinement, culture... But this type of culture infuriates most people. And I am not talking about having read more books or being more knowledgeable. What I mean is a certain *art de vivre*, at least on the surface... This is what separates the different social classes in France and makes life so pleasant. But we must face the facts: these very characteristics also make the class distinctions hard to bear.

In the United States, wealthy people have the same way of life and the same concerns as the population as a whole. They may be greater consumers, far greater than people who have less money, but their aspirations are basically no different. Everyone expresses himself in the same way and, in exchange for the loss of elegance, the Americans have also avoided a class struggle. The American model has no social distinctions.

I also believe that in any country where people desire to do away with a cultural past, the class struggle fades away more easily. In the China of the 1930s, for example, there were differences between cultured people and those who were not, while in the 2000s, those differences have disappeared. And yet, inequalities exist that are as least as great if not greater than in 1930, but they have become much more bearable because there was an attempt at acculturation. In a country like Switzerland, where everyone is middle class, there is no class struggle either. There are some cultured people, others who are not, but they all live the same way, even though they have different interests and varying amounts of money. But this does not make them jealous, for no one pretends to be anything but what they are.

It is the aristocratic ideal that makes life pleasant but it also makes social relationships difficult. And in France, there is another factor: the *parvenu* who aspires to a better way of life and irritates everyone. If aristocrats are often better accepted in the provinces, it is because they have an understanding of others. Within themselves, they might sense their differences, but superficially, they live the same life.

The American model comprises freedom, a longing for wealth, the desire for personal success, a certain harshness in social relationships and a merciless war to ensure that the strongest wins out. This Darwinian model has conquered a large part of the world. It is in the process of triumphing in Russia, Eastern Europe and China where it will adopt far more savage forms, that is to say purer forms, but only because those countries have to make up for lost time. When a thin layer of Socialism is placed over Capitalism, it slows Capitalism down. As a consequence, this can only be done once a certain level has been reached: up to that point, it is not as easy. But I believe that the Capitalist system remains the very best to assure economic development. After some resistance by traditional society, Japan has also succeeded, thanks to this system, there is currently no other convincing model.

The Marxist social model failed and no one outside of Europe is enthusiastic about Social Democracy because it is weak, relatively inefficient where the economy is concerned, and perceived as the product of aging societies. It is not a flag that people often wave for the very good reason that it doesn't work! And everyone knows it... In the Arab world, the population does not believe itself to be either ready or capable or, consequently, eager to adopt the American model. They feel too disorganized, too subjugated beneath a religious system to participate in Capitalism, and, to them, this religious model is the only possibility. The United States is indisputably a country where people feel immense pride and great patriotism, a country that has known how to integrate people from all over the world better than any other. The fact that there was a black Foreign Secretary like Colin Powell and that today Condoleezza Rice holds the same post, that the head of both American Express and Time Warner were also black, and that this is considered normal, represents a prodigious success: even more so since half the black population in America today belongs to the middle classes. Their advancement since the 1960s is extraordinary. And there is something thrilling about the greatness of this country, about its dimensions, its landscapes, its cities, its ability to create a world out of nothing. Here is the Tower of Babel...

The display of social solidarity on public holidays in the United States delighted me immediately. Thanksgiving dinner is not a totally private affair, as Christmas is in France, but a public communion with all of America. In the same way, on July 4, the Americans all do the same thing, from the top to the bottom of the social ladder: they have a picnic at the seaside, and it is an emotional, joyful day.

Perhaps you cannot really understand the United States unless you realize that it is a very religious country, mainly Protestant, where it is virtually incomprehensible to state you are an atheist. And democracy plus Protestantism, as Tocqueville very clearly demonstrated, results in the tyranny of the law.

Justice is stronger in the United States than compassion. Everyone is presumed innocent until proven guilty; but once found guilty, there is no forgiveness.

The shadow of the law hangs heavily over this society. There is no way out, no discussion possible and no leniency to hope for. Catholic ideas of redemption are not appreciated in the United States. If you are guilty, you are guilty. You can begin your life again afterward but, in the meantime, there is no place to hide. Paradoxically, people in America have more freedom than anywhere else and yet more people go to prison there; people can be successful more than anywhere else and yet, more than anywhere else, you can be fired, ruined and can lose everything overnight.

One day, when I was first head of Lazard in New York, I couldn't manage to get in touch with one of my partners, so I let his secretary know I was not happy about this. He phoned me saying that she'd told him he had been fired. No one in France would have ever thought such a thing. To put it another way, there is complete brutality in people's reactions. This brutality encourages a kind of intoxication, which, like any type of intoxication, has something pleasant about it. Being able to change the world around you goes to your head... The successful come from the most unlikely social milieus. I have had partners who were the sons of immigrants who didn't speak any English and washed dishes in restaurants. I had one whose father was a Jewish shoe salesman in a black ghetto in Philadelphia, and another, a black man, whose mother was a cook in Atlanta. Each of them hoped to live the American dream.

Thanks to this, there is very little jealousy in the United States. People do not believe in the class system and they are right because, deep down, for better or for worse, aristocratic distinctions do not exist there.

Americans never forget that they exist primarily because of what they do and what they represent. Unfortunately, this behavior has reached France where I have noticed more and more people at dinner parties talking about their professional activities. This is inappropriate because you can only talk about such things superficially. And the spectacle of these men showing off in order to hide their anxiety has something pathetic about it... I find it rude to talk about work outside the office, including within the family, even more so since it is in a vague way. I have never allowed myself to do it. It is the opposite of conversation! If you confirm your doubts people will conclude: "He's headed for disaster!" And if you never share your uncertainties, you seem smug. It is irritating to see these men getting all worked up; I walk away and find someone else to chat with, preferably a woman. Yet I admit to feeling sympathy and even compassion towards these men because I know how difficult life can be for a man. Women are more refined and I feel almost humiliated by the transparent behavior of men. The result is this arrogant attitude which runs counter to what made the *salons* of the seventeenth and eighteenth centuries in France so charming. At the *salons*, which were hosted by women, people were invited to discuss interesting subjects with one person at a time in a way that was entertaining, without ever talking about oneself or being boring, and it was unheard of to raise the issue of one's personal problems. This art consisted of making the person you were conversing with shine in the best light possible, with an ease of conversation, regardless of their intelligence, beauty, wealth or status. This was an exquisite challenge, and there are still some traces of it left today in Paris... But I am conjuring up a world that has all but disappeared and is rather difficult to access, as newcomers are not really welcome. In this world, an exemplary loyalty in camaraderie reigns; I dare not call it friendship. After a rather long stay in New York, a fellow from that circle once turned to me and said: "Have you been ill with the flu?" because, even though he hadn't seen me for three years, I was still so present in his mind that it didn't matter. And another person said: "We never see each other but that is of no importance. The less we see each other, the closer friends we are!" And it was true. This type of intimacy has always pleased me, but it only exists in Paris. Does it still exist in England? I don't know. In any case, it is absent in the United States. What is wonderful in Paris is that you are not judged for what you are. You are acceptable because you are accepted. No one looks any further, which is very relaxing and rather magical. Practicing this very French art of conversation with women adds a great deal of pleasure to life for a man.

Any joke that is somewhat risqué might shock people in the United States but the same taboos do not exist on both sides of the Atlantic. American society is much more puritanical than French society, even though, sadly, French society is becoming more like its American counterpart in this respect. On the other hand, it is probably more difficult to oppose popular ideas in France, where pressure to conform is stronger than in the United States.

The illusion of perfection is gaining ground everywhere. This is why people are getting divorced for the slightest reason. In the United States, people are constantly flabbergasted when they think: "But it's unimaginable that someone or other did that." It's getting to that point in France. In the past, you might not have approved of certain types of personal behavior, but you knew they had always existed and that some people would always behave in those ways. You weren't necessarily in favor of it, you might not have even been able to bear it, but that's how it was. And people were more tolerant of behavior that only affected the people involved, even if that behavior was morally unsound. Today, people are surprised by it.

People's private lives are being made public more and more, including in France, which is not a good thing. This encourages indignation and the false innocence that is unbearable in the United States seems to be taking hold in France. In England, it's incredible: the hypocrisy regarding scandals is extraordinary. Not a day goes by when you can't open an English newspaper without reading about absolutely unbelievable sexual crimes, described with delight and horror, intended to be scandalous. This tendency is spreading to France, unfortunately... Where sex is concerned, nothing shocks or surprises me. My father always used to say: "You can marry just about anyone, but be careful whom you sleep with." Take a man in his prime with more or less unlimited wealth, put him in a city where he is all alone and anything can happen. I don't see why anyone should be surprised or scandalized by that.

It is always shocking to see the press accuse the victim of a crime, as was the case with Édouard Stern. The revelations in the media upset me because of my daughter, who loved the man deeply, and because of my grandchildren, to whom he was an excellent father; I have nothing to say except that I consider all of it a rather inevitable mess... The fact that Édouard died a violent death did not surprise me. He was an extremely intelligent and attractive man, but rather destructive as well as self-destructive. In addition, he had a taste for danger for danger's sake firmly fixed within him and this led him to take great risks in every situation. It seems obvious to me, on the other hand, that there truly was a victim in this story, and that victim was Édouard Stern. Forgetting this fact seems improper.

In France, I am struck by the startling contrast between a very beautiful country, well cared for, with an extraordinary transportation system, magnificent cities and villages, a marvellous way of life – from the art of dining to the art of looking after oneself, conversing, growing older – and the powerful sense of boredom, jealousy, dissatisfaction, moroseness, rudeness, as well as the hostility that taints personal relationships and makes life unnecessarily but tragically uncomfortable.

Effort counts for nothing; everyone is – and should be – helped by the State, work is not appreciated, demands are endless and virtue seems a thing of the past. You get the impression that the French take comfort in individual moments of happiness while the rest of society is in chaos. Now, given all the advantages and beautiful things that exist in France, it is not normal to be so depressed and unhappy there.

Hope, which is humanity's prime mover, seems to have deserted France. Nevertheless, I am not fundamentally pessimistic. I know very well that this situation is not irreversible and I believe that this tendency will one day be reversed. All the lack of appetite and admiration for success will return, and it won't be that difficult. The big French companies are international and very successful throughout the world, which is extremely positive. In fact, they have already broken through. Should the French economy be run by the French? It really is of little importance if a French company has an American or a Japanese running it. What is essential is that these companies are part of the impetus and dynamic economic expansion that will give hope back to the French. In any case, history shows that companies always return to their country of origin.

In the United States, hope exists... what counts is their taste for innovation and a stimulating environment. The Americans are impressed by the success of someone like Bill Gates. The same kind of person in France would have to hide. An enterprising Frenchman is at odds with French society: the fabric of society does not support him, he is not admired and, if he earns a good living, he is not highly regarded. And so he goes somewhere else. A hundred thousand Frenchmen already have successful careers in Silicon Valley and many hopeful young French people are leaving to go abroad – to England, China or the United States. It is believed that injustice is the most serious factor in discouragement because it creates differences between people, but there is something even more serious: a lack of hope. To my mind, true satisfaction for human beings is only possible if they can aspire to improve their lives or the lives of their children.

In France, people believe that the State can do anything and, in general, the men who lead the country live in a world outside of economic concerns. Their political role accords them privileges that place them, in fact, outside the system of Capitalism. They work an enormous amount, but nothing encourages them to accept the real world just as it is and where you pay for your privileges. They are despots who want to construct another world, an artificial, ideal world actually, where the laws of economics do not apply. To tell the truth, very few people want to believe in the economic virtues linked to Capitalism: competition, lower taxes, reduction in the government's rate of expenditure, privatizations, the possibility of firing people. The freedom to be enterprising, hard work, social mobility, opening up new horizons, all these things have been proven possible in England, the United States, China, India... In France, you reward corporatism and reject what is blatantly obvious.

To put it another way, the beautiful idea of justice that consists of wanting the maximum equality between men is overrated. You can impose all the progressive taxes you like to correct human nature but what counts, first and foremost, is giving people back their hope. The young people from the poor suburbs are potentially a great source of talent in France and some of them are good examples of how to succeed. But there are not enough of them and they are not well known, which does not encourage others. The United States cultivates such examples as role models and there is a great deal of solidarity within these communities, whether they are Jewish or black. And this changes everything, since the real question always remains knowing how to give people back their hope.

I can understand how a Frenchman might not agree with a particular aspect of American politics, but I suspect that anti-American feeling is just an excuse to people who refuse to see the world as it is, that is to say, a modern world, made of international competition, increased mobilization in most countries and a taste for success. And I am quite afraid that, in reality, this anti-Americanism might symbolize a refusal to be committed in the real conflicts in today's world and the hope that by showing tolerance, others will come to be tolerant as well. Anti-Americanism is a serious illness in our society, but probably less widespread than our leaders think.

On the other hand, I can only despair at the strength of anti-French feeling that has become more or less unanimous throughout the United States since the French stand against the war in Irak.

Apart from the question of whether the French position was justified, people felt there was intentional hostility and indifference towards the United States, which, in the eyes of the Americans, had been subjected to an act of war on September 11, 2001. More than a betrayal, it was a question of a hostile attitude and, given the historic role of the United States in the wars in Europe, it seemed completely undeserved. France was not the only country opposed to the intervention in Irak. One might very well be against it, but it wasn't necessary for France to use its veto or to campaign within other countries to oppose the United Nations and the United States. France could have taken a more reasonable, justifiable position towards a friendly country by stating that it would not participate in something it considered a mistake. Moreover, that was not at all what France seemed to be saying. Rather, the general impression was "let's all unite against this mad, imperialist country". This type of behavior is very common in certain French circles where a large proportion of the elite actually believes that they should be given credit for adopting attitudes that affirm they are different. What was revealed to be disastrous was *the way* this was done, even more than *what* was done. While it is completely reasonable to disagree, going so much further to express one's disapproval seems unreasonable to me because we are part of the Western world, and that world would be extremely weak without the United States. To shoot down the United States is to act against our own interests.

Moreover, our enemies know this and they are not wrong: in the end, they put us all on the same side. This is why there is a confirmed alliance between Al-Qaida and the Algerian terrorist groups who are against France.

Apparently, military intervention in Irak was not the best response to the war against terrorism. But it is nonetheless true that the country and the government that fight the war against terror most is the United States and the government of George Bush. And all we actually know is that if this battle is not fought, we will be defeated, unless you believe in being naively optimistic, which would mean saying that if we are very kind to our enemies, they will end up liking us... I do not think that the solution is to appease staunch enemies.

Reflections on a Professional Career

I had always known that I might one day become the head of the Lazard Bank, but I came to realize that I was actually the only one who had no doubts about the matter! In 1977, when I arrived in New York to become the company's senior partner, I understood that it was a very improbable idea to everyone, even a joke, to have appointed me, me, a privileged young Frenchman, to run Lazard. It was symbolic of the extent of André Meyer's despair. Meyer was head of Lazard in New York at the time and couldn't find a successor; the business was headed for disaster! I was again described as a "privileged Frenchman" in the 1990s when the press became more critical of me. The Americans feel no jealousy whatsoever if money is earned. On the other hand, anyone who has the audacity not to fit the generally accepted idea of his place in society is considered privileged. And, therefore, in a certain way, he is envied. Every career is full of pitfalls and errors, and I had my share like everyone else. Yet, even at the very worst moments as senior partner of Lazard, I never thought: "Now here's proof that I can't do this. 'To get to where you're going, it's best to know where you're headed.'" For a long time, I thought that I had invented that saying, but then I discovered it came from Seneca! I realized that people never ask themselves this question. They forge ahead as quickly and forcefully as they can, but they do not know which path they have chosen and never wonder if it is worth their trouble. Did I wish to see Lazard expand or not? Was our presence desirable in a certain country or not? In every case and at all times, knowing where I wanted to go seemed crucial.

"I was handed my responsibilities too early," my father told me, "and I hadn't been taught the basics. Learn your job before trying to do it." This is why I spent two years working in other banks in New York: one year at Brown Brothers Harriman, in 1955, and the other at Lehman, in 1956. At Brown Brothers Harriman, I was responsible for studying the credit lines of small import businesses and to determine, by analyzing their balance sheets, if they were going to lose money or be in a position to repay what they owed. They weren't very important tasks, but they taught me to understand the realities of a company's financial situation. At Lehman, they didn't really know what to do with me, so I was given the annual reports of large American companies from ten years earlier and asked to predict what would happen to them. I sweated blood and tears over those files before realizing that it was idiotic because, in 1948, the Korean War had changed everything. I thus acquired the certainty that you should never believe in projections.

At that time, I did everything necessary to learn the profession. I went to the analysts' meetings at Lehman where there were impossible personalities who fought in the most terrible way, but I kept out of it... I would go home every evening, thinking: "Yet another day when I've done nothing." So for two years, I was deeply bored but... I had learned a lot! In 1958, I passed an examination as a financial analyst and went to London to spend three months at Lazard. Then, when the interest in Algerian oil was spiralling out of control, I found myself back in Paris. I spent three months at Eurafrep, a company that carried out oil research and whose President was René Mayer, a former Prime Minister of the Fourth Republic. After spending three more months at Lazard in Paris, I rejoined the bank in New York where André Meyer was then director. I worked there as an employee at first, until 1961, then as a partner. I learned my profession by osmosis.

André Meyer helped and supported me a great deal while I was gaining experience. He was a very complex person, an extremely intelligent man, amazingly active and with unbelievable drive. He worked an enormous amount and had a high opinion of both his profession and the firm. He drove himself and controlled everything because he didn't like to delegate. None of his acquaintances, whether they were ordinary people or very famous, visited New York without stopping in to see him. First of all, he demanded it! And he was extremely attentive and courteous. There wasn't a single person in the company who didn't get a phone call from him if they were ill. Added to this, he needed reassuring so he was hungry for compliments and loved being charming, especially to women. Everything he did was accomplished with a mixture of affection and great passion. His horrible temper terrified everyone, even the company's rivals, which was not without its advantages! I knew certain executives, whose

REFLECTIONS ON A PROFESSIONAL CAREER

banks were more important than Lazard at the time, who would concede when faced with the almost physical violence of his reasoning and who ended up agreeing with him, out of fear.

I had to learn how to stand up to him, which wasn't in my nature, given my habit of being polite almost to the point of self-effacement. Whenever I went home angry at night, I would try to confront him the very next morning, which taught me to say what I had to say quickly, rather than continuing to worry in silence. If you wish to reproach someone for something, or feel suspicious or resentful, you mustn't let the situation drag on. I believe in the magical power of words; they create the truth. When people allow themselves to get carried away with extreme verbal displays and lose their heads, something always remains in the air... So it is destructive to blow up and it is not necessary to get angry. Even if words can achieve a lot, they can't do everything and, without inner force, they are nothing. The strength of words matters because the phenomenon of the group leader is akin to animal behaviour, where sheer strength counts at least as much as the spoken word, that is to say, everything that comes from character, aura, influence and the power of conviction gets incarnated in one individual.

With these resources, I took on the challenge of a career in which I would be responsible for the most diverse sectors, all the while realizing the difficulty involved in working between the New York, Paris and London branches of Lazard. They all functioned rather independently and did not see that certain matters could be dealt with synergistically. Now that globalization exists, this might seem obvious. At the time, however, it was not. If I always desired to merge them, it was because, to me, they formed a single entity. Basically, the structure of the different Lazard branches has always been rather complicated, but very interesting, because it was a question of building something along the lines of the European Union, where people were united in their concerns, their hopes, their professions, even though they remained different according to the country they were in.

By observing André Meyer, I came to understand two simple but essential practices in running a business: the necessity of giving a reply within 12 hours and always being available. It is pointless to wait any longer than 12 hours. If you have no opinion within that amount of time, you might just as well leave it to chance whether you say "yes" or "no". It also makes the people you work with feel very secure. If André Meyer received a memo in the evening, he made a decision the next day. I taught myself to do the same. This is not always without risks. One evening, he asked me to purchase some shares. The next day, he changed his mind, but I had already started the process. "If a partner of Lazard has made a commitment," he said to me, "he keeps his word." No reproach whatsoever. He once wanted to take on someone rather elderly as a partner. He called him in for a meeting and announced what he intended to do. The person was rather stunned. "I am very honoured," he replied. "Can I think about it?" "Yes, of course," said André Meyer. "It's an important decision. I'll phone you in two hours." I recall meeting a client in New York with the team from the office and a banker from another firm to study a case. "We need to think about all of this," André Meyer concluded, "We'll discuss it again in a few weeks." The others had only just left the room when he turned to us and said: "I want the plan tomorrow morning." You can't take your time in business.

The second principle is your duty to be available to your team. You must appear to be happy to listen to a partner, including on the telephone, even if you are in the bath or at dinner or very early in the morning. André Meyer wanted to know everything, all the time, night or day. I remember calling him once at some ungodly hour and saying: "Please excuse me; I hope I'm not disturbing you." "You only disturb me," he replied, "when you don't call me." I have never forgotten that and I have always made myself available to my partners all the time, wherever I might be. At the time when telephones didn't work as well as they do now, for a long time this restricted my travel to distant places for a long time. Before going somewhere, I would get information on how the phones worked because I didn't believe that I had the right to go anywhere if it wasn't possible to reach me quickly. Work was at the heart of my life and I can honestly say that for more than fifty years, there was not a single hour when Lazard was not my central preoccupation and, at every moment, the foundation that underpinned my deciphering of events.

Before becoming senior partner of Lazard Paris in 1975, after my father's death, I was aware that those years were the easiest of my life because whenever I had made silly mistakes, I was protected by the power of a patron: André Meyer in New York, Pierre David-Weill, my father, in Paris. From 1965 to 1975, I had the extreme pleasure of living in very close contact with my father. We would go to the office together in the morning; I liked chatting with him while he was getting ready and I even continued to call him Papa at work... Those ten years were enormously enjoyable and rewarding. I was thirty-two and, thanks to André Meyer, I already considered myself more or less educated about business. Did I feel that I was young? I don't believe in youth or in old age... In any case, I no longer felt the need to have a mentor.

I therefore had the joy of a relationship with my father that was relaxed and unrebellious. He led the kind of life that appears to be one of complete ease and privilege but, in truth, he had to deal with many problems. First, in 1932, the year he married my mother and just before I was born, a branch of Lazard in London had lost a considerable amount of money, so much money that my father and André Meyer, who were junior partners at the time, were in the red. Although backed by more senior partners, they were in debt and made nothing until 1938. In addition, after having fought in the army, my father had to cope with the "Aryanization" of Lazard. He managed to give depositors their money back and ensure that his employees would find work elsewhere. Before the United States entered into the war, France was considered an occupied country, and therefore the enemy, so he had problems with what was then called the "*deal with the enemy act*". Then he had to get along with André Meyer, who was a very talented person but who was also very difficult and jealous of him. After the war, my father reopened Lazard's Paris office; it had been closed down and he had to completely rebuild it. From a professional point of view, his skills were relatively unrecognized; all the credit went to André Meyer. So the primary lesson that

REFLECTIONS ON A PROFESSIONAL CAREER

I learned from him was courage. And good humor: he never complained. He also had a great deal of common sense when it came to business, and by that I mean that he could intuitively distinguish what was true from what was not, though the false was often discernible by its sheer excess. Very often, people spend time deciding between two solutions when they shouldn't make any decision at all. "The most important thing in life," my father used to say, "is what you do not do."

Today, people talk about nothing but how to manage a business. The truth is that you need common sense. In order to succeed, you need anxious vigilance, determination and good judgment in business matters (that is to say a mixture of knowledge and instinct that might also be called intuition, if you consider intuition the result of experience that ultimately appears to be natural). To be specific, it is necessary to know how to compare the reality of the moment with the possibilities that come with time and be resolute in decisions. Anyone who has a true desire to do what he wants to do will have followers and will be able to convince those who disagree with him.

If, moreover, he has a bit of distance, that's even better, especially in a management position. I have known people who had two of the three qualities: anxious vigilance and determination, but who thought, for example, that the Internet boom would last forever. Now this was a result of bad judgement... I have known many booms: in France, the oil boom in the 1950s, the conglomerates boom in the 1960s. And I experienced the boom in the housing market in the 1970s. The economy is made of a succession of spiralling prices followed by great slumps.

Yet it is sometimes at the very moment when everyone is discouraged that you mustn't be, and when everyone else is getting carried away, you should be most cautious. I remember Antoine Bernheim, a partner at Lazard, who had very sound judgement. Our London branch had sent him insurance company executives wanting to buy buildings in Paris in the 1970s. Bernheim told these people: "Do nothing; the prices are too high." Lazard London was terrified by this reply. And Antoine was right: three years later, the market collapsed.

In addition, it should not be forgotten that every time someone has announced a miracle, disaster is not far off. In this respect, I have always thought that being confident of the greatest success is one of the major signs of financial collapse because a taste for speculation goes hand in hand with excessive optimism. In fact, all companies, States and individuals wish to believe that they have found the philosopher's stone and have forever become part of a virtuous circle. Such misplaced vanity induces a feeling of superiority, which in itself is a precursor of future problems. This is why the Japanese believed that their social structure would lead them to permanent economic development, but it did nothing of the kind. The Mexicans thought they had the recipe to allow their economy to take off. Southeast Asia felt superior to the rest of the world. Even the United States thought they had found the secret to the creative innovation of infinite wealth. The China of today is a model of growth and confident it will eventually take its place as the world's top economic power. None of these beliefs would exist if they were not at least partly true. But when excessive confidence leads to extremes, that very confidence is a sure sign that problems will follow. However, if confidence lasts a rather long time, the choice is difficult. It becomes a question of either letting opportunities go by out of caution, or having faith that you are sufficiently alert to know when to jump off the bandwagon.

For better or for worse, I have often been correct in my judgment much too early. Around 2000, the financial world in America experienced a period of prosperity, when people earned an enormous amount of money, followed by a very serious financial collapse. Both the newspapers and financial institutions demanded what companies ended up doing: no more dividends three times a year and no more getting into debt. Directors gave in to popular demand and even achieved the results that were asked of them. Anyone would think that earning money had become a normal and natural right!

The specific nature of the economic world is that it consists of booms and busts, because it is at these critical times that opportunities arise. A series of these – a new process or invention – engenders a surge of activity and hope. Now, everyone wants to find something that will make a difference, whether positive or negative for that matter... People involved with economics have an unfortunate tendency to forget the norm; they get carried away because they are either too optimistic or too pessimistic. However, it remains a well-known fact that the day the morning papers announce: "the stock market is doing fantastically well", it's all over. And when they say: "disaster at the Stock Exchange ", that's the time to buy. Journalists reflect the tone they sense from the general public. The people involved in economics generally

A TASTE FOR HAPPINESS

believe that tomorrow will be more or less like yesterday. Good judgment consists of thinking about what is normal and what is above or below than the norm. If the situation is worse than normal, it will improve; if it is better than normal, it will get worse. It isn't all that complicated. But judging how long it will take for people to understand the situation is actually quite difficult.

One should neither put trust in the blinding light of success, nor completely yield to the latest craze, and it is important to realize that economics contains hidden truths. This is why property is good value when it has a 10% return but is too expensive when it yields less than 5%. That's simply how it is. And every generation forgets that. When it brings 3%, people say: "But it will increase, it always has, it doesn't mean anything", while it is known that if it returns 3% one day, it will drop; when it brings 10%, it will go up. These are inviolable rules. My father knew this. In the same way, if someone said to him: "Everyone is doing it", he would think: "If everyone agrees, it must be foolish." And when it was foolish, he spotted it immediately. Whatever happens, it is necessary to keep your goal in mind and never lose sight of common sense.

People often talk about the mystery of Lazard. It isn't exactly what people think... "The secret of Lazard", André Meyer would say, "is its secrecy". At least, that's what people said he used to say... And it is true that the virtue of a small company like Lazard depends on the discretion it owes its clients. They certainly do not desire premature publicity about hypothetical deals that would not perhaps take place if announced too soon. But how have we

REFLECTIONS ON A PROFESSIONAL CAREER

succeeded? Simply through the strength and reputation of the Lazard name and by being sufficiently respected that our opinion is sought on important issues, even though we are a small enterprise. Because on an international level, a business that employs two thousand five hundred people with limited capital truly is a small enterprise.

Therein lies the true mystery, and it has intrigued and irritated many people. To paraphrase Stalin, the competition has always had an anti-pontifical reaction, if I can put it that way, and would ask: "Lazard has how many divisions?" They would end up concluding: "Be serious, Lazard doesn't count; I can't even understand why you're going to talk to them." And they very often contributed to our mystery by *not* talking about us. Our colleagues almost never mentioned us when they wrote articles on general banking. It was a Freudian omission: they were incapable of seeing how a business that was so different from theirs could actually exist. We had been involved in numerous important deals that had been reported in the press, but there wasn't a single article on Lazard that didn't end with: "Can this go on? How?" And always with a recurrent question: "What miracle is keeping them in business?" We remained very reserved, sought to establish the best possible teams and had the will to succeed.

Then a true phenomenon took place in France: it was a matter of historical chance that Lazard was not nationalized in 1981. We found ourselves with a monopoly in our profession in France, which can be pleasant and exciting initially, but which turns out to be bad in the end because there is only one thing left to do and that is to do less, and there is something disagreeable about any hegemonic situation. In 1978, we told certain Socialists: "Study the Lazard bank and you will see that it isn't really a bank but a financial services firm, with close contacts in England and the United States. If you nationalize it, you will be nationalizing nothing because a financial services enterprise that helps other businesses is made up of people, and you would be depriving the French economy of a useful tool. Consequently, it would be wise to study the situation very carefully." After consulting the French Communist Party, they replied: "You're right; you won't be nationalized." Obviously, we kept this in mind and the danger passed without us worrying about it anymore. When the Socialists came to power in 1981, we reminded them of what we had been told. Certain people who were close to François Mitterrand were convinced by our arguments. At the time, I was advised to become an American citizen to avoid nationalization. I found that idea improper. In the end, the law stated that if a company held a billion francs on deposit, rather than the five hundred million francs previously set, it would not be included in the nationalization plan. As this was our case, we were spared. This was why Lazard was not nationalized, unlike the majority of the other banks.

In the years that preceded my birth, there existed the widespread myth of two hundred families who formed a Capitalist hydra that conspired to oppress the people! But the economy functions according to rules that are not political. For example, there is no real conflict between profit and employment: there is convergence. In other words, when someone says: "You mustn't shut down this factory", that doesn't mean anything, unfortunately, because if it continues to lose money, not only will it close, but the other factories in its group will also close or they'll be taken over by someone who will shut them down. A company cannot survive if it does not make a profit. Therefore, the idea that there might be two kinds of businesses, those that exist to make profits and those that exist to provide employment, is absurd.

There is another world-wide phenomenon I am convinced will happen: just as less than 4% of people in France are farmers (even though that figure was 33% when I was a child), in the future, 4% of the population will be workers, and manufactured goods will be made by poor countries in Asia, or India. The writing is on the wall. This might be upsetting, but don't forget that manufacturing abroad brings development to other countries which, in turn, will be able to buy services from our countries, and all of this increases general economic growth. But whatever happens, it is inevitable.

Economic history teaches that every time you erect an artificial barrier in order to get back on your feet and play for time, sooner or later it comes crashing down. And when it does, it causes even more terrible problems than if it had never existed. Of course, one must try to foresee solutions as far in advance as possible and create jobs, but, unfortunately, the anxiety that exists about this can only lead to more rapid relocation precisely because there are no more new jobs. If you cannot close a factory in France, one thing is certain: another factory will not be opened. The leaders of industry to whom I listen think this way: "All right, it's very difficult to close a business in France. I will try not to do it, but I'm going to set up my next factory somewhere else."

Consequently, this only exacerbates the problem. Such safeguards have been tried, but they simply they do not work. They hold back the inevitable march of time... and make it even more inevitable.

My father always used to say "a Capitalist regime is superior to a Socialist regime because Capitalism can operate with a high degree of Socialism, while Socialism cannot accept any Capitalism". I am in favour of a free market, but I do not oppose the rules that guarantee competition... It is equally legitimate to wish to set up protective regulations at certain times. In Europe, for example, the car industry was protected from Japan for a while. This was only acceptable because the desired goal was freedom to import. To put it another way, it is possible to conceive of temporary safeguards that can sometimes be useful. Certain imports end up destroying the local economy, agriculture in Africa, for example, or sending old clothes, which prevents the development of regional industry. As far as I'm concerned, the individual's imagination is stronger than the collective imagination, and everything that can be done to allow the imagination to reign is desirable!

I hold the certainty that there is no future without Capitalism. In truth, only two systems exist: a system that spreads poverty and a system that creates wealth. I am not saying that the system that creates wealth cannot be complemented by social measures, but, fundamentally, the only system capable of creating wealth is Capitalism. So unless people prefer a fair system under which they will become poorer on a long-term basis to economic growth that is more or less fair, Capitalism is the only solution.

REFLECTIONS ON A PROFESSIONAL CAREER

Believing that all we need to do is to distribute the existing wealth in a better way in order for everyone to be well off seems unrealistic to me, because I have never met anyone who did not strive to improve his own position or that of his children. In China, meteoric economic progress is leaving a large portion of the population even worse off. Moreover, the growth of the part of the population that is progressing is itself very unequal. People may say that this situation is unbearable and want nothing to do with it. Progress is also unequal in developing countries, not just among individuals, but even among different age groups. In China or Russia, it is the twenty-five to thirty-five year olds who are becoming greater consumers and seeing their lifestyle improve, which cannot make people of my age very happy! When you question these people, they are quite optimistic, while almost everyone else tends to be discouraged. Progress, therefore, reinforces numerous unavoidable inequalities. Of course, these can be remedied because you can put the brakes on and accelerate at the same time, just so long as you don't brake so hard that you actually stop the car. But when it comes to an economic system, Capitalism has completely triumphed. I have never thought for a moment that any other system could provide proper economic results and, what's more, it's never been known to happen...

A system of state control might claim a certain number of glorious results, or supposedly glorious, in its name: the Egyptians built the pyramids, Nazi Germany created a powerful army, but this type of regime never led to prosperity. Prosperity has a name, and that name is Capitalism.

A TASTE FOR HAPPINESS

Modern Capitalism created a continual movement of flexibility in all aspects of social life, and this was an enormous change. No society benefits from innovation for more than a few brief years because the desire for new ideas and products is stronger than ever, and this results in successes that happen more or less by themselves but which are often fleeting. Consequently, the item created and the people hired to manufacture it can lose their usefulness far more quickly than in the past. For this reason, today's economy consists of incessant rough patches that make it very chaotic on all levels and difficult to bear for everyone. Retired people want to invest without any risk, but that is not possible; the workers do not want to lose their jobs, even if they have to retrain; a company director knows that his business might go bankrupt at any time, even if his yearly results are good. We are all moving at a furious pace, and the idea that China might wage war against the United States or Europe is not true: the Chinese too have joined in the perpetual, rapid movement of economics and, therefore, benefit from its advantages and suffer its disadvantages. In any case, I am a staunch Capitalist and even one of those rare individuals – at least in Europe – who has always believed in its ultimate victory.

In France, resistance to change is very strong. But it is necessary to realize that every time innovation occurs in one area, the consequences of the changes it brings with it are felt in others. A new product competes with the old one, which must become obsolete; that's just the way it is. If the old one were kept, it would, by definition, become more and more costly because no one would want it anymore and, in the end, it would be prohibitively expensive.

Certain electronic component factories that opened less than five years ago have already closed. In this field, as in others, the unit price drops by 25% every year. It is a formidable race to perform well and produce something new, and this brings with it the shutting down of companies that manufacture outdated goods. It is impossible to conserve what is old and create something new both at the same time. You could be philosophical and say: "Perhaps it would be better to be poor and happy than rich and miserable", but this is the kind of world that Rousseau imagined and which undoubtedly has never existed. I am not sure that today's western world is happier, but I am convinced that it provides living conditions that are more conducive to happiness. People live better and longer; they enjoy improved health, have leisure time and can hope to see their material situation improve. All of this has a price, and that price is change. And it is very difficult to change. In my profession, it is an obsession: "Are we going to survive?" This question exists in every field. You cannot give a client advice that goes against industrial or financial logic. It would be meaningless to tell a client: "Do nothing; you'll still die, but it won't happen until later." That isn't our role, nor anyone else's for that matter. I am very respectful of the facts: we live in a society that is developing at a dizzying pace, for better or for worse, and probably more for the better.

It is essential to adapt; there is no way to avoid it. The State, in its sovereign wisdom, can decree stopgap measures to lessen certain effects on individuals, but that is very costly and it is society who pays. The great illusion, in France in particular, is that "someone else" can pay. At certain moments in history, people said:

"The banks will pay", without understanding that the money in the banks consists of the deposits that their clients entrust to them – and I would be surprised if they wanted to hand over their money so we could spend it! "The State can pay" is another aberration because the State is the people. So any social measure is good on condition that someone can pay for it. An attempt was made to convince the French that it was in the national interest to exert less effort and that it was possible, for example, to share out the work. The truth is that the more people work, the more they provide work for others. To claim that increasing the amount of vacation time forces other people to be hired is quite simply untrue. There is less unemployment in countries where people work a great deal than in those where they work less. Linking personal interest to communal interest has resulted in disaster because people were allowed to think that it was virtuous and politically correct to work less.

For a long time, France was an agricultural country where nothing changed... The majority of people of my generation, in France in any case, but not at all in the United States, remember it nostalgically and think of the modern world with terror, saying over and over again: "Where are we headed? What is this destructive world of globalization?" In fact, it is nothing more than the reflection of popular will, the will to have a better way of life.

Lazard's position in France as a monopoly in the 1980s greatly contributed to substantiate the idea that we were rather powerful, a kind of Second Ministry of Industry. Before that period, in 1970, I recall an important industrialist came to see me. "I would like to work with Lazard", he said, "This must come as a surprise since I already have two other bankers, but I need someone discreet. I do not wish to acknowledge my concerns to large institutions. They would begin to doubt me and I want to be able to confide in a private company." I remember that day very well. "This is the beginning of a great phase for our company in Paris", I thought. And it was true. I also recall another industrialist who visited me, around 1985. "I've come to see you and it bothers me", he said, "because I have no choice." In fact, there wasn't anyone else to go to. Then I thought: "A prosperous chapter is closing and a new one beginning, and things will get more and more difficult." And that is exactly what happened in France. The parameters of this phase are fixed in my mind, in a rather precise and amusing way, by these two visits.

In the United States, the mystery of Lazard was a result of our very existence. Historically, the position occupied by the company in terms of the number of transactions was not very great. However, when you looked at the most important transactions in the country, we were high on the list. This fact added to the mystery... In truth, it was a matter of a specialization like any other, just as someone might run a luxury boutique rather than a grocery store, but it added to the bank's mystique, which is not such a bad thing, as long as it doesn't go too far.

In this respect, we managed to avoid two temptations: the press and politics. Our cautiousness concerning any involvement with the press was owed to experience. Before the war, Lazard owned shares in a newspaper called *Information*. It was later apparent that the paper's stance on foreign policy was clearly pro-German, which upset us terribly, but there was nothing we could do about it. I therefore learned very early on that you shouldn't get involved in a newspaper, and I remembered that lesson. Nor was it our place to make public any political convictions. Each of my partners had his own opinions, and I didn't necessarily know what they were. Sometimes, in the course of a conversation, I would realize that the person I was speaking to was a very close friend of someone or other. Some people had left-wing friends, the majority were rather right wing, but we never got involved in politics in any way whatsoever.

To keep going is difficult, more so today than in the past. Company directors burn out far more quickly than before: they currently have fifteen years to look forward to, not thirty. In addition, the pool of people who can understand what a private services company really is – a mixture of drive, caution, conservatism, innovation and the desire to survive in the long term – is much more limited than in the past. Most people who currently go into banking often do so in order to quickly be successful and then get out, without any concerns for the future of the company. In the past, on the other hand, people chose this profession with the long term in mind and because they desired it. In truth, what set them apart was that, in addition to talent, they had a taste for it. To be a good investment banker, you must recognize that you are not a specialist, but you are expected to make judgments about a wide variety of activities and problems. You do not have to be involved, however, with everything you would need to know if you were an industrialist. In other words, it is a virtual profession, and thus modern. It is also necessary to have the desire to convince, never to be satisfied, to

REFLECTIONS ON A PROFESSIONAL CAREER

always want to start again, not to feel depressed by rejection, but to bounce back and move on to a potential new assignment. A kind of somewhat masochistic energy is therefore necessary because, whether you like it or not, it is a profession in which you have to sell yourself. When you are turned down, it is you who are rejected, your mind, your ideas, your beliefs... and that is quite unbearable.

Add to this the fact that the partners at Lazard – that is to say a limited number of individuals contractually linked to one another and the sum of whose talents is the basis of the company – commit everything they own personally. Now, even if you remain very cautious, the amount of money necessary for success tends to rise, and private fortunes diminish because of taxes and inflation. My father always used to say that France contained no rich people except the *nouveaux riches*, in the sense that, anyone who hadn't rebuilt his fortune since the advent of inflation, no longer had any money; that much was obvious. In this respect, there is no difference between someone who bought bonds from the City of Paris in 1913 and someone who bought Imperial Russian bonds in 1913. When you combine the two factors of taxes and inflation, the result is that the dependence upon private money becomes more risky. I have never been surprised by problems. The life of commercial enterprises is part of History: it is intense and moves quickly. Industrial or banking dynasties do not last for long. If you look at the list of people who were wealthy in France in 1900, you can see that only four or five are still on the list today, and this is true in the United States as well. A royal dynasty can last for several hundred years, but if a business dynasty lasts a hundred and fifty years, it's a miracle. I have always known this.

I believe that you go from success to success until you finally fail, but that is no reason to stop trying.

To succeed at Lazard, you had to know how to take off by yourself. The English have an expression for this: you had to be a "self-starter", with no money and no one's help. It was up to each person to create his own clientele and invent ways to carry out his profession with a state of mind that was closer to professionals than to office workers. Unfortunately, this is in the process of changing.

As for me, I might as well have been a Redskin when I first arrived in Paris from New York in 1965. I was utterly astonished at business lunches during which no one discussed anything before coffee, and at the stubbornness of a certain number of company directors who were totally inflexible in their ideas. My father once invited me to lunch with an important steel magnate. At the end of the meal, I risked saying to him: "You know as well as I do that the steel business seems to be going badly at the moment. Don't you want to diversify a little?" He turned towards me and replied: "See here, young man, I am in the steel business and from Lorraine." He went bankrupt. Actually, he didn't, but his successors did...

It was at this time that I began watching the prices of shares being traded on the Paris Stock Exchange to see which ones were interesting, looking at them as from another planet. And that was how I found myself involved, on December 21, 1968, in the Exchange Offer of BSN – the predecessor of Danone – on Saint-Gobain, which caused quite an uproar. Saint-Gobain embodied the respect owed to traditional French Capitalism; we

REFLECTIONS ON A PROFESSIONAL CAREER

were amongst the few people to support a more upsetting, anarchic, yet efficient type of Capitalism, and which was set to destroy the Institution Saint-Gobain established by Colbert under Louis XIV. Strangely enough, politics got involved. During the 1960s, there were still traces of the OAS (the illegal organization that backed French rule in Algeria). A bomb exploded at the home of Antoine Riboud, the CEO of BSN. I received death threats over the telephone. I remember very clearly having replied: "Thank you very much" to the person who was speaking. He called me back immediately thinking that I hadn't understood. But I didn't really see what else I could possibly say... I didn't want to hire bodyguards and was already sceptical of those protective measures that can in reality work against you and which, in any case, completely destroy your daily life. To tell the truth, I would prefer to be assassinated in peace...

At the time, Saint-Gobain caused BSN's offer to fail by asking numerous European companies to buy shares, which it promised to buy back afterwards – something that would obviously be illegal today. But from that moment on, Antoine Riboud became the champion of modern Capitalism in France, more energetic, more socially concerned, more open, and enjoying the success we all know he had. From a failure, he knew how to create a great success, and that failure was carried like a kind of banner! I will also say that Lazard remained BSN's banker. Afterwards, we became Saint-Gobain's bank too...

I believe that I was not wrong in understanding what made up a private enterprise, as the Lazard Bank was. It is an independent company specializing in providing advice to enterprises, and I am certain that it will engender others along the same lines. Moreover, it is doing just that. Why be independent? Giving independent advice to decision makers can only be done by people to whom this is their primary profession. And by people who are independent themselves, not employees of a large group, because there is the risk of a conflict of interests, while in a small consultancy firm, nothing is more important than the advice and the client. So it is better to remain free. What is involved in advising businesses? Take the case of Danone. It is not typical, insofar as it is rare for a banker – me, as it happens in this instance – to have such a close relationship with a client who became a friend. Despite the failure of the Exchange Offer on Saint-Gobain, there was no buying or selling of shares by Danone without a discussion between its CEO, Antoine Riboud, and myself, for I personally dealt with his affairs. He wanted to buy Kronenbourg and I encouraged him to also buy the company Européenne de Brasserie, because to my mind, and to his, it was better to be first than second and to have a dominant position in the field, despite the problems involved with Européenne de Brasserie (a much more complicated and diversified company than Kronenbourg). Next, my role was to help with this acquisition, that is to say, to enter into negotiations, determine its value and work out how to pay for it. When Antoine Riboud's company changed into a food-processing industry, I believe that I played a part in his decision to get out of the plate glass business. (He was still manufacturing windows, windshields for cars, etc.). Could he become a food-processing company of the first order while retaining a considerable investment in another sector? I didn't think so, and I told him so.

An investment banker becomes personally involved in the conception of a company and the hopes of his client. When a company is not doing well, it is also his responsibility to say what is saleable or not, while the client might wish to sell the very thing that is not marketable because no one wants it, least of all him! Our role is similar to a medical specialist who makes a diagnosis and prescribes the treatment.

In truth, there are two bad methods: one by which bankers always say "yes" and the other when they always say "no". Always saying "yes" works rather well; it is the method used by people who admire the initiative and the intelligence of their client and who make themselves appreciated by saying: "Now that's a good idea." Consequently, they are quite well regarded. The opposite method impresses the client who thinks: "Now here's a banker who cares about me and won't push me into making stupid mistakes; on the contrary, he'll try to hold me back." Obviously, a good banker is someone who doesn't always say either "yes" or "no".

This profession has changed a great deal. Today, people seem to prefer quantity to quality. "How many transactions of this type have you done? How many of your people will be working on my affairs? What kind of research can you get published? How much money can you invest in my company? How efficient are your teams?" These are the kinds of questions you are asked when someone is choosing a banker. There are all sorts of criteria that tend to lead you away from what I call "untainted advice". Add to that another important factor:

"Are you less expensive than the others?" If you had cancer, you would want to see the top specialist and know who was on his team, what facilities he had, etc. Most important, you would want to go to someone you could trust.

I had the same problems as André Meyer in finding a successor. He had tried everything. He appointed someone from outside the company and more or less made him president. He had tried to convince Felix Rohatyn to direct the company. Felix was a wonderful banker who later became American Ambassador to France, but he had no desire at all to take it on. In the final days of his life, my father told me: "Do not try to run the New York office while André Meyer is still alive, you'll get crushed." But I could see that the company was failing. It made me think of an elevator: I was sure to step into it one day, but where? Would it be on the second floor, the ground floor or three floors below ground? When I had the impression that it had dropped to the ground floor, I told myself that I had to go. I had been approached by certain partners in New York who confided in me and admitted that things were going very badly: "Mr. Meyer is not at the office much anymore (he was very ill), and he's trying to run the company by phone, but everyone is getting demoralized; people are starting to leave and more and more of them will go. You must come." In fact, André Meyer himself finally asked me to come to New York. We were co-senior partners for a year. It was difficult for him to no longer be the person who made the decisions. I already realized that but, today, I understand it even more... He didn't come in very often, so I had to rush over to his house for hours at a time, give him reports, discuss things and, at the same time, try to run the company. It was very difficult... I never fell out with him but, in a certain way, to punish me, he resigned after a year, which was, in fact, liberating. And he died the following year. I respected André Meyer a great deal; nevertheless, his was a reign of terror. Once I saw through his system, I no longer had to suffer it because I understood who he was. Since I have no talent for guilt, I never succumbed to the kind of masochism he so brilliantly knew how to instil in his colleagues: they were often shattered by things they believed to be entirely their fault and would leave his office beating their breasts.

Today, when I think about the place of the Lazard Bank within the context of its history, I cannot help but consider the model of what a private bank is, and the extent to which it is susceptible to external events. In a company made up of individuals, like Lazard had been, there was no personal ownership. You only owned a bit of capital and the right to profits. When you left, you were given back your capital and you no longer had a right to profits; you surrendered that right. However, in 1964, when I decided to incorporate the London branch of Lazard with the New York office, I inadvertently opened Pandora's box, because part of Lazard London belonged to Pearson, which was a public company, that is to say a company whose shares could be bought and sold. When it came to buying out Pearson's shares, the buyer was a French public company, Eurafrance, which was controlled by Lazard's senior partners. Quite naturally, Eurafrance considered that it should have full ownership of the rights it was acquiring. This meant that, if necessary, it reserved its right to profits when it withdrew, instead of conceding them, as is the case with a private company. Basically, this meant that, at that moment, Lazard ceased to be a private company, that is to say a company where the partners' only rights are the rights to profits and where there is no ownership in the long term. Out of fairness, we extended the same right to the other partners working in the company, thus paving the way for going public, because, once shares can be bought and sold, you end up a public company.

When Lazard began being traded on the Stock Exchange, it required the company to change in order to become a model of profitability compatible with a public enterprise in a way that was in opposition to the principles of a private company. This seemingly logical transformation contradicted what had been the spirit of Lazard, where the partners had been financially liable on all their assets: while they shared in the losses and profits, but they retained no share in the business once they left.

A financial establishment listed on the Stock Exchange obeys a different internal logic, which comes down to the satisfaction of public shareholders in the short term. Now, it is important to know what a shareholder in a public company thinks: "What is good for my investments in the next six months?" Whereas a partner, as I understand the term, asks himself what is good for the company in the next ten years. It is of a different order, with a different capacity for taking or not taking risks. When you are a public company, you might be led to take more risks because you have to provide instant gratification and, at the same time, you must be less patient when faced with adversity. For example, you might be obliged to merge with a competitor because times are bad and people are worried. You are therefore subject to the situation of the shareholders rather than the situation of the company. Almost all of the financial institutions listed on the Stock Exchange had to change profession. You therefore find yourself at the mercy of a collective judgement that is not necessarily correct, for I do not think that the stock market is always right.

Between Bruce Wasserstein, the current director of Lazard, and myself, there was no personality conflict, despite what has been written in the press. I recognize his many virtues: he loves the company; he is passionate about Lazard. He has a great deal of authority, energy, optimism, and he understands the profession. I knew all of this and was not at all surprised by these things. But what I hadn't really seen was that he nonetheless gambled with the company during a difficult period by spending a lot of money, not his own money, but my partners', and mine and that was an unpleasant surprise. Nor had I realized exactly how afraid of me he was, which he told me during the only interview that we ever gave together, when Lazard was first listed on the Stock Exchange. Consequently, he did not wish me to maintain any role alongside him. In this, he was a victim of the propaganda that I would not hand over any power to anyone. In reality, I had tried, but I took back power because it wasn't working. People thus concluded, not illogically but incorrectly, that I didn't want to hand it over. To tell the truth, if I had handed over the company to anyone before Wasserstein, it would have been a catastrophe... The fact that I loaned and then took back power was actually an attempt on my part to do something for the company, much more than for myself. If

I was prepared to try it with Bruce Wasserstein, it was because I had made the decision to do so.

We had different views on the future of Lazard. We do not have the same instinct for money. He believes in <u>value/prices</u>; I believe in recurrent profits. Take any company at all and let's say it is making money, about two billion, and it is worth twenty billion. You could either think: "The goal is to earn two billion and five next year", or "What is important is that the company is worth twenty-five billion next year." One person is concerned with the profit the company makes, the other with its appreciation in value on the Stock Exchange and the careful management of its image. These are two different perspectives, even though they are linked by what is known as the "multiplier of profits". Imagine that a company sells its shares at nine times its profits, another at twelve times and yet another at eighteen times its profits... It happens that Lazard sold at eighteen times. It might be more interesting to some people that the company is worth eighteen times its profits rather than increasing those profits by 10%... These two elements are not necessarily contradictory, but the emphasis is different.

To Bruce Wasserstein, it is practical to be a public company listed on the Stock Exchange – it is not a matter of an ideological vision to him – and that allowed him, on the one hand, to restructure the expenses of the firm that had become burdensome as time passed, and, on the other hand, to satisfy the people who owned part of the company, not only the original partners but, more importantly, also those who worked there. Was this change avoidable? I have no idea. Would I have chosen that particular moment? Probably not. Can I understand why a great number of partners wished it? I understood enough to accept it. Did I wish to be a simple shareholder in the company? No. I was willing to change if people wanted it, but on condition that I leave. Which is what I did.

CEO/Director/Head of Lazard

And if I had it all to do again? I would do it just the same. "He tried"– that is the epitaph that can be written on my gravestone. I find that expression beautiful in English, so concise. I often said to myself: "Next time" – in another life – I might be a good dancer. "Next time", I'll be able to ski. "Next time..." I don't believe it, but that is of no importance... I could have made something else of my life, but would that have actually made such a great difference?

As CEO, I always found it liberating to make decisions. When I am handed a problem, I have to immediately classify it in one of three categories: "unsolvable problems" which, consequently, I would be indifferent to and not trouble about, "problems easily solved with a 'yes' or a 'no'" or "problems that require reflection", which I so enjoy solving. It pleased me that my "yes" or "no" was final and could not be contested.

I have never spent much time considering what people might think of me and I have been lucky in life, very lucky: no one says anything very bad about me to my face! In any case, it is not good to say: "yes, perhaps", or "no, but then again, why not?" You end up being embarrassed or living in the land of "maybe". Whatever the case may be, it was necessary for someone to be in a position to make decisions... While I was CEO of Lazard, that person was me.

Nevertheless, I have always maintained a certain detachment in that I never believed for a moment that what I was doing was truly important. Being CEO of Lazard is wonderful: you find yourself surrounded by intelligent people and privy to all sorts of information, and that was exciting to a curious person like me. It is a career that can be enjoyable and very profitable, which is not without its advantages to someone who spends a lot of money... But I have never really believed in power. Not in my own or in anyone else's.

I feel sympathy and even compassion towards powerful people, in particular those in the political domain, members of government, for example, and for the gap that exists between who they are and their responsibilities. They have often chosen that particular path and desired it, but nevertheless... it is difficult. I am rather benevolent, which is another form of respect. I take powerful people as they are and feel grateful for their efforts. It sometimes happens that I am almost too indulgent, believing that they shouldn't be condemned too hastily because they have been virtuous enough to at least try. I give the benefit of the doubt to anyone who runs a country or a business since they have shouldered the weight of the illusion of power. They are used to other people accepting their superiority, but they are just as helpless as everyone else. When I look at a President of France, I know very well that he is as unhappy as the rest of us... For a while, the way others see him gives him power, but this is just an optical illusion, though one which has, it is true, real influence.

To my eyes, power is nothing more than the reflection of the opinion of others. It is other people who grant you the power that you do not actually have. In truth, such admiration for a leader and the quasi-religious element attributed to a CEO or a President, is nothing more than one of many social conventions. People force their accepted ideas on others; they see you as they want to see you, but I do not feel that I have changed very much throughout my life because I have never confused the significance, that is to say the prestige of my situation, with any personal importance whatsoever. Since I never defined myself by my position, I don't find myself inclined to inflate my own importance, but neither do I believe in the importance of others. Obviously, it is a greater fault to be impressed by yourself than by others.

While I have always respected rank and responsibility, I have never been impressed by them. I have what I call the "complex of a Royal Family"! A Royal has an obligation to live up to his position in every situation. It is a question of being polite and showing interest in whatever people say to you. It is a matter of respect towards everyone and for each individual because no single person is more important than anyone else. It is not virtue that makes kings: their birth imposes a certain type of behaviour that is necessary to fulfil their destiny, which is to be who they are. Attentive, courteous, approachable.

Whether they enjoy it or not is irrelevant; it is a question of duty. In addition, a king is no more intelligent or admirable than anyone else. He is a king; he has a certain position, that's all – and it's not his fault!

As for me, I consider myself a conscientious craftsman. And through a combination of true modesty and rather great pride, I have rejected all of the rumpus, more or less concocted by the press, which creates the appearance or illusion of a personality. Since I left Lazard, I do not wake up in the middle of the night thinking: "Damn, it's terrible, I have no power anymore!" If I do happen to wake up with a start, it's because I had a nightmare... about being back at Lazard! If people considered me as a symbol of a certain type of power, success or way of thinking, I had no desire to take any notice of that. I don't believe in it. It only reveals the human need to idealize certain people by endowing them with prestige or power... I rejected that idea precisely because of my pride, which makes me feel disinclined to believe I am more than a good craftsman. In truth, I would feel a lesser man if I accepted the perception of others. When I meet people who embrace their social image, I do not like it very much: I think less of them because they are reduced to the role they are playing. And so, I removed myself from the person I played. I do not know him and do not wish to know him.

I am not, however, at all modest when it comes to the quality of judgment and influence that Lazard has had as a whole. In a world of several billion inhabitants, it gave me great joy to realize that a few hundred people at the heart of a business of only two thousand five hundred employees could make a difference in grasping a situation. Consequently, I have always been aware that we were a rather special elite. It carries a certain weight if you have good judgment and are sufficiently independent, and by that I mean that you are not necessarily looking at a situation from the point of view of self-interest. If I rejected any personalization of power of any kind, it was because I believed that a collective intellectual power existed at Lazard. Moreover, that power was never used politically, although it was preferable to know the political players in order to understand what they thought of an issue or a project, even if it were simply to remain informed. As for me, I never liked rubbing shoulders with politicians while they were in power. I prefer meeting them when they are no longer in office because they are freer and are often very interesting. Perhaps this is also somewhat snobbish...

Since Lazard was an enterprise made up of partners, each one had his own idea of his profession and how to carry it out, and so some people cultivated those in power and were closer to them more than others. However, the greatest links were established with high-ranking officials and senior civil servants who sometimes viewed the company as complementary to their role.

My partners were entirely responsible for the matters they handled. From time to time, and usually at their request, the partners would send me to negotiate. Sometimes there were deals that I handled personally, so I would have to see a top official or the Minister of Finance. A certain number of CEOs think they can do things better than other people and when the most important affairs come into play, they step into the limelight. That was not the case with me. And that is why such strong personalities were able to develop at Lazard.

The idea of developing what is commonly called the "thirst for power" has always seemed absurd to me. I have never experienced either the desire or the necessity of doing this, which was probably a drawback... and my most obvious professional shortcoming. People who identify with what they perceive to be their power want to affirm it and set it upon a solid foundation. The best way to succeed in establishing power is by coming into contact with people who play what might be called a comedy of roles: they all know each other, recognize each other, make use of their relationships and quote each other. And, the world being the way it is, this is very useful because, on the one hand, it provides access to people who, by definition, also believe in their own power and, on the other hand, it creates the illusion that you are powerful, because you can slip things into the conversation like: "When I spoke to the Prime Minister last week over breakfast..." Suddenly, people are thinking: "Goodness, I'd better pay attention." And it happens everywhere but it is staggering how, especially in France, mentioning important State officials changes the perception of the person to whom you are speaking. When I say that it is a disadvantage not to have played that game, I am speaking from experience.

When I consider how much André Meyer used the art of knowing people, of being known, of getting close, liking and being liked by the "world's most powerful people", I cannot say that the effort he made was not useful in carrying out his profession. It was very useful. But

I never practiced that art because I did not wish to and did not have the time. I have lived in several countries, which limits a person's time, especially when you take into account the time differences and work to be done. You can't face spending your evenings, which are fewer the more you travel, trying to get other people to notice you. I completely refuse to feel remorse or regret about this because such feelings serve no purpose. However, if I had one piece of advice to give to a young man starting out in this profession, I would tell him not to imitate me, because playing these roles counts for a great deal. I even consider myself almost a miraculous survivor in not having failed by behaving as I did, as it isn't common. Would I have been wasting my time at those parties? Time is never completely wasted. It may be exhausting, but it is essential.

As sceptical as I am, I nevertheless behaved as if I were not. And I never allowed my scepticism to alter my behaviour in any way, which gave me a certain freedom in the business world and is essential to avoid making mistakes. This is why I almost always saw red when someone told me that they could not have done something differently. Nine times out of ten, it was a question of something truly stupid. Just like the adage "Everyone is doing it". That is a true warning sign and nothing more than an excuse for every excess. For a very long time, I was completely free... when I was about to take over as Manager of Lazard in New York, I told André Meyer: "If you want me to behave like you and not like myself, I'll get the next plane back to Paris, I really won't mind at all." However, after twenty-five years, I had the impression, rightly or wrongly, that I was much more responsible for the fate of

CEO/DIRECTOR/HEAD OF LAZARD

Lazard because I knew that my decisions would affect its future, and so I was far less free at the end of my career than at the beginning.

There are not thirty-six thousand ways to run a company, there are only two: through terror or through consultation. In the short term, terror is more efficient. André Meyer used that method with thoroughly convincing results, but I have never been able to do it. Certain people would not perhaps agree on this point. Let's just say that people do not greatly dislike intimidation. A large part of the domination practiced by some leaders consists of making their colleagues feel guilty, each of them, personally. It is not difficult to benefit from this; it is even the entire basis of sadomasochist relationships. So the colleague excels and is grateful to his boss, primarily because he did not feel he was capable of accomplishing what was expected of him and yet managed to achieve it. And as a result, his self-esteem is satisfied. To terrify is to be loved! "I'm off to war to kill everyone. Whoever doesn't get out of my way had better watch out," said Père Ubu, one of my favorite literary characters. He also said: "Mère Ubu, you look very ugly today. Is it because we have guests?" All that makes me laugh. When you like Alfred Jarry, you cannot seriously terrorize people for very long!

Unlike the use of terror, which causes a virtually instinctive reaction on the part of the victim so that he excels, persuasion in no way builds a person up; if he feels manipulated it is only because he is being convinced to re-examine his own logic. And, in fact, it was the contribution that each individual made to the company's success that was important in carrying out my profession.

The drawback of the relationship based on terror is that it is simplistic and cannot evolve in a complex way. On the other hand, a relationship based on intelligence can be multi-faceted, but it is too detached, and people resent you for it.

Many mistakes occur in the business world, particularly today, when people do not respect the facts and mistake appearances for reality. A company president may seem to be successful if he buys other companies, but he may not be managing them properly. Everyone thinks he is creating wealth while he is actually only acquiring them for less money than their value on the Stock Exchange. Or he makes people think that he carried off an important deal, even though it doesn't make any money. He forges ahead all the same because it is fashionable, because he has convinced the public and because he thinks it will bring a lot of profit. But you mustn't get the timing wrong! Nothing is more important than being sure that the basic tenets of your business dealings are sound. You cannot compensate for a loss simply by pulling off some big deal and thinking that this will make up the difference in some fantastic synergistic way. I suppose that this might work at times. But even if it does, I find it too unpleasant and intellectually dishonest to be acceptable. It is a never-ending battle to respect the facts, the people and to earn respect. It is necessary to continually put things back in their correct place and calmly say: "You have a right to your opinion, but you do not have the right to deny me mine or to deny my capacity to have a different opinion." When you are thinking of the future, the risks a company can run are greater in the end than the advantages.

But just as someone will walk to within five feet of a lion, it is human nature to wish to defy danger. Man's condition, in fact, is to ignore the social consequences of the acts he commits if he believes them to be private rather than collective when he is perpetrating them. And this is what happens in many instances of breaking the law. How could a great personality have embezzled one hundred thousand euros – when he was being paid one million five hundred thousand euros – knowing that it might destroy his life? He was aware of it, but he had come around to the idea that it was a matter of a private act, neglecting to make the connection between his actions and society. This proves man's deep need to sporadically behave in an anti-social manner, and this need wins out over the caution that generally inspires his actions. We see this happen all the time and yet are always surprised by it. How could such a respectable man believe he could use confidential information for his own profit? The repetition of this type of action in various sectors shows that it is not a question of unusual behavior. We are forced to recognize that it is natural for human beings to behave in anti-social ways and to take reckless risks that are disproportionate to the anticipated pleasure or profit such risks might bring. People need to feel alive. They have great difficulty in living by the rules. Little by little, they end up fearing their own boredom even more and, from time to time, they think: "I don't care", and commit the act; they have stopped thinking. Then they do something stupid or criminal that is pointless. Nevertheless, it should not come as a surprise.

I have never believed in democracy in business, nor do I believe in the efficiency of any kind of collective management. I am not a fan of committees. I have always known that you must attend them with a preconceived opinion in order to guide them and, as a matter of fact, to win out. On the other hand, I have always believed in one-to-one consultations because they can raise issues you may not have considered. Until 1990, we succeeded in attracting people with very diverse talents and none of the partners chose to leave to work for another bank. I have known men who had extremely good instincts. They might have had a definite opinion when they came in for a meeting and yet, right in the middle of it, they would suddenly change their minds and, as it turns out, they were right to do so. This is just the opposite of those who believe that they have meticulously examined every detail of a deal and who still wind up making foolish errors because they do not have all of the facts at hand in order to make an informed decision. So they say to themselves "Well, we'll see what happens"... André Meyer thought that you could never count on making up for lost business and my father believed that most any deal could go bad. What is essential is to have good business instinct. One of my partners used to say: "I hear with perfect pitch, but I sing off key", his way of saying that he could sense what was going to happen but that his business acumen was not equal to his intuition. It is enjoyable to hear things correctly – to understand the issues – but a banker, just like a political leader, must make decisions.

It is even necessary to be wary of an overly-complicated way of thinking because you should arrive at simple solutions while never forgetting the lesson taught by experience: fools are generally right. People who are not very sophisticated do not burden themselves with subtleties.

They have no gifts whatsoever, don't think very far ahead and make hasty judgments that ignore a person's most important qualities; yet their rather superficial impression of people is usually correct. This is annoying because, while they simplify matters hugely, they can immediately see that Mr. X would not be right for the deal or that he can't be trusted. It is sad to admit, but that's the way it is.

Intelligence is mainly a pleasant art. It has its little uses; for example, it helps you to predict the next move before other people. However, in order to succeed, you must first have courage, and even a kind of nerve, so you can make a name for yourself. A businessman with whom I worked once told me: "People who have not inherited money have to borrow it to make their fortunes." The real qualities needed to succeed are a vigorous life force and leadership skills, so you can lead your troops to victory. If you are not headed for disaster through a lack of intelligence, you can still end up there through pride or smugness, which are, moreover, often linked to one's life force. An exalted idea of yourself and what you do is a vice; sometimes it has good elements, but pretentiousness is almost always fatal. Seeking revenge, believing you are stronger than everyone else, ignoring the facts, all these things lead to disaster.

Power is taken; it cannot be given. And this must be clear to everyone. My father died in Paris, in January 1975, and I went to Sicily for ten days after the funeral. I remember thinking, and this is not insignificant, that it seemed obvious that I was the one who was going to take his place. Why? The folly of youth... Months later, I found out that during the brief period between my father's death and my return from Sicily, the partners had not considered this such an obvious fact. But since I had taken it for granted, no one objected; the obvious became the imperative! Before I went to run the bank in New York, the situation was different. I was less sure I wanted to do it and I enjoyed living in Paris a great deal. A certain number of partners campaigned for me. "We have no choice," they said, "There's no one else; we have to try him out; we have to reassure him; he has to be the CEO."

And that was how it happened. With time, experience confirmed in my mind that power cannot be shared. You either have it or you don't and if someone contests that power, it is better that someone else takes your place. Diluting power is pointless. I allowed myself to be convinced of the contrary but it didn't work, and I knew it wouldn't, although I continued to hope I would find a successor through that process. But I didn't.

My role as CEO consisted of motivating the partners, inspiring them and freeing them from the burden of running the company. I took responsibility for those things and, consequently, they had ample free time to look after their clients. André Meyer always used to say that being a professional banker consisted of "a series of kicks in the behind, sometimes crowned by a success"!

My function was rather like the role of an orchestra conductor and consisted of providing the impetus for the entire group. A CEO has to be a rallying point. It is through contact with the CEO that people feel part of a group and not alone with their problems. It is with the CEO that they sometimes come to recharge their batteries, receive congratulations or even to be criticized. And he is the one who must set the tone, the atmosphere that is unique in every company, and he is also the person who maintains or alters it. I considered myself a unifier who disseminated information. I couldn't help but get involved in all the paperwork that passed through the office and this irrepressible curiosity has never left me. I have had the great pleasure of being, if not at the heart, then at least part of one of the important hubs of information. Because, in truth, that is what an investment bank is, first and foremost: a concentration of up-to-the-minute knowledge which, by definition, is fleeting, but whose very value is its immediacy, even though it is backed up by previous experience. During the rare times when we held plenary partners' meetings at Lazard, I was always deeply impressed by the sum of knowledge assembled there. When a matter is being concluded, it is in the client's best interest to have access to numerous facts in every area. What are the anti-trust, fiscal and financial policies at the time? What is the true state of chemistry, insurance, oil, banking, Information Technology and all the various components of the economy? And also, to a certain extent, what is the true situation of a particular country, region or institution?

You might say that I lived with my partners around the clock and that we were almost a family, which is a relationship that is simultaneously more and less than a friendship. The beauty and nature of a family is that you never wonder if they are friends! That's how it is. I made a great effort to bring together Lazard Paris, New York and London because I felt that these companies formed a whole. In 1984, when I physically combined them by taking over control of Lazard London, I realized that the partners didn't know each other, while I knew them all, even the ones who worked for us in Milan, Frankfurt, Madrid, Tokyo... It was a long, drawn-out process to integrate the partners who all came from different places but I felt it was very important to do this while simultaneously conserving their individual national identities. But if you are going to treat people as partners, that is as equals, then it is necessary to speak with each one of them about their lives, their aspirations and their remuneration at least once a year. This last point is essential because Lazard paid its partners a percentage in relation to the company's profits. The percentage of the global profit was fixed annually for everyone according to the business they brought to the company, and this could vary from year to year depending on individual results.

I always tried to ensure that the remuneration reflected objective criteria as far as possible, which is terribly difficult – and I did this with extreme care and scruples. I had to meet with roughly one hundred people at least once a year, without counting those whom I had to see several times. And there is no getting away from the fact that people find nothing more interesting than themselves. Consequently, they bring a good deal of self-interest to these meetings that you must share with them. In addition, you can be certain that if someone says: "I have something important to tell you", he is going to talk about himself...

I do not regret these meetings, even if they were exhausting, because I learned a lot about people's reactions, their strengths, their weaknesses, their concerns, their aspirations and what motivated them. I realized that people are not motivated by the same things in different countries. For an American partner, things have to be *fair*. It is quite easy to tell him: "You haven't done very well this year. I'm sorry, but that means you'll be earning less next year." If he thinks that you are right, he will accept it. On the other hand, it is very difficult to tell him: "You have had wonderful results this year, but I can't give you much of a raise", because he will consider that unfair. A French partner is more concerned with the respect you show, to him and to others. And, in this case, such respect is translated into money. He would tell you: "I know that Mr. X did nothing this year, but it would nevertheless be embarrassing to give him a cut in percentage." What is implied is that he is too important and you would be humiliating him in the eyes of the other partners. Even if I replied: "Listen, in order to give you a raise, I really have to give him less", because it is a question of a percentage and there is only one hundred percent, he would insist: "No, I would rather that Mr. X also be compensated." And he himself would ask for respect, that is, I would have to reiterate: "I know very well that it's thanks to you that we have done this or that and, moreover, everyone appreciates it." When determining their percentage, this element was another factor, apart from the strictly economic considerations. The criterion of fairness is far less important. These differences between the French and the Americans persist, even if they aren't as pronounced today. In Britain, I was astonished to discover that one of the major passions of the English is happiness. Those partners tell you: "Yes, it would surely be financially advantageous to take on Mr. X, but I don't think we'd be happy with him". In other words, working together in harmony seems an essential element of the English character. People are very dedicated, take a great deal of trouble and are proud of what they do, but their primary concern is not to be in an unpleasant environment... Alas! Even though this might be an admirable criterion, the result is that there are no more English banks! In the City, in London, there are practically no more Englishmen left. There are young Americans, French, Germans and Italians who are taking their places. So the English banking system has to sufficiently cross-breed with foreigners in order to survive!

Being aware of these different types of behavior proved very useful, but there were limits: I refuse to allow myself to get as emotional as the person with whom I am speaking. I rarely get angry; I am not easy to get close to, by choice, but this can also prove a source of difficulty. In addition, I was surprised to notice that, from the 1990s onwards, years that were more difficult for me, I was described as very authoritarian. This must be due to the slight distance that I have always maintained towards others. People deduced that I felt superior or that I wasn't really interested in them, which isn't exactly the case: I just do not wish to get too close.

I accept that I am somewhat snobbish: I prefer that people do not like me rather than me not liking them. To be hated is not very pleasant, but it is far more disagreeable to hate others because that involves and damages you far more than being hated. Being hated is a problem to the person who hates you; it's not really your problem. That said, I have very sharp common sense that means that I like my friends and not my enemies and, to me, there is a great difference between people who wish me well and

CEO/DIRECTOR/HEAD OF LAZARD

those who wish me ill – and who might even like me if they didn't hate me so much.

I have been very keen to retain my independence in relation to anyone and everyone. This was crucial for me and was non-negotiable. It is not in my nature to be one hundred percent committed to a specific path or person. Yet I stay very involved and am extraordinarily stubborn, so I am prepared to do my utmost so that my relationships with the people I know remain intact and do not flag. The people who try to get close to me, however, receive an unwelcome gift: I do not wish them to be dependent on me, because I want them to be free. When people experience solitude, as I do myself, it can be troubling. My past and my lifestyle mean that I have to accept the fact that I am not like everyone else. My children and close friends have accepted this. We may sometimes pretend otherwise but the truth is that people like me, who live the way I do, are not like everyone else. Some find my freedom annoying, but I don't care: that's their problem, not mine! Am I egotistical? Probably... I believe that until you experience misfortune, you don't believe it will ever happen to you.

I was told that I had no fear because I was the boss, but the truth is that I was the boss because I had no fear. I have always known this and I was surprised one day to hear an Indian businessman, a specialist in computer programming in India whom I didn't know, quote my own saying to me. It is probably a question of temperament... What is called "courage" is nothing more than a personality trait which no one should take pride in: it is physiological. We have no choice, and it is true for the majority of a person's basic character, just like beauty, intelligence or cheerfulness. You are born that way... So we are left with behavior, for someone might be handsome, intelligent, cheerful... and either a hoodlum or a person of stature. On September 11, 2001, when the World Trade Center was attacked, I would have surely remained in the towers. I was in New York in my office on the 62nd floor of Rockefeller Center when I witnessed the disaster firsthand, and I was one of the last three people to go down into the street. When you think about it, it does absolutely no good to give in to panic; you simply have to think about the situation for thirty seconds to understand what is happening. My absence of fear in the face of danger, therefore, is due to a slight delay on my part. I react more slowly than other people and I have noticed that there is a period of time between what I am feeling and the consequences that result from it. And I also do not wish to add to the chaos. One day, I was on Concorde when there was a serious technical problem – one of the engines seemed to be exploding – which my neighbor, who was an airline pilot, told me. I thanked him for the information and continued to read the Chinese novel I had started. When we finally managed to land, he asked me why I had remained so calm. "It was out of my hands, there was nothing I could do", I replied, "So it was pointless to get upset". I refused to allow myself to get involved in an exceptional event over which I had no control.

In the banking world, on the other hand, I was able to act and react, but I always made a conscious decision to avoid getting upset when problems arose. It is possible, for example, that people publicly reproach you for a decision that you believe is fair: you chose one client over another and they claim that your choice was not only a mistake but that it was based on personal considerations. If it's nothing of the sort, you mustn't waste a moment worrying about it; it isn't a real problem. However, this profession is risky, especially because there is often a very fine line between what is considered legal and what is not. One of the difficulties of the business world is that certain transactions that are legal at a certain moment in time may be deemed illegal afterwards, and penalties are sometimes retroactive. After the fact, a court might decide that you set up a particular financial arrangement in a way that you should not have. Now, in today's world, there are no mistakes: there are only crimes. You are either guilty or innocent. Before acting, you must therefore have good sense in order to judge whether there is a risk of anything illegal. Sticking to what is appropriate, honest and meaningful is not enough because you can never know if everything is being done by the rules.

When you are in charge, it is very difficult to know everything in detail and a system of checks, which is necessary, generally proves to be completely inefficient: it does not take human error account into and dishonesty is not always discernible before a crime is committed. Being on the lookout for such things is thus a constant concern for a director. Moreover, it has been proven that when under pressure, because of greed or fear, some people are suddenly tempted to go down the wrong road. As for me, I have always believed that people whom you have shown your trust have less desire to betray you than the others. The risk is infinitely reduced, I would say to one chance in ten; otherwise, it is one chance in three. So I trust people and judge them by their actions. It also sometimes happens that someone comes to see me to tell me that Mr. X is behaving badly and cannot be trusted. If I know how he has behaved for ten years and it isn't badly, there is no point in paying attention to the fears being expressed and my opinion will not change. When someone does something foolish, you should be indulgent. I just think: he made a mistake.

However, even if it has taken me a long time to realize it, today I know that you can never change anyone. Certain people convince themselves that, in the end, they are no worse than anyone else and that it is not necessary to be better. They think that everyone does what they are proposing to do, convinced they are not really as corrupt as other people and that they have the right to do it since... everyone else is doing it! It is often so subtle and happens so gradually that getting used to doing the wrong thing is insidious. But they end up crossing the line of honest, basic, simple morality without even realizing it. It is imperative to think in order to have the courage to say "no" in time.

It can also happen that you are unable to prevent someone from drifting, sometimes because you think that other people know all the details of a situation better than you. The fact remains that you mustn't believe that something does not exist just because you can't see it, while simultaneously remembering that the only possible policy is one of trust. In the world of economics, as in politics, it is therefore necessary to set yourself moral limits. If a company is living a lie – which might happen if it feels forced to by circumstances – and it rushes into speculation that it shouldn't, you must try to stop it. It is good to be flexible, but it is necessary to be rigorous. The only way to do this is to make a conscious decision to remain indifferent to the consequences of your position. In other words, you must have the courage to oppose or dissociate yourself from general opinion and from those who cross the line.

Running a bank demands extraordinary effort for one simple reason: it is a competitive world in which there are many intelligent people, even if some of them allow themselves to be carried along by events or what is fashionable. The difference between two intelligent people with the same level of education is the quality and quantity of their efforts. The one who exerts more effort will dominate. Being the CEO of a bank thus demands total commitment. To run this type of business, the impetus you must provide to others is moral as well as physical. You find yourself surrounded by colleagues who generally display good will but who are lying in wait to catch a flaw, a weakness, something illogical or shaky that they can detect in you. The CEO of a bank constantly finds himself in the position of a lion-tamer surrounded by wild beasts. And this is more and more obvious with each generation since there is so much less corporate loyalty.

When I speak of physical effort, what I mean is that you can't even allow yourself to get the flu. You are obliged to always be present and in the best physical condition. One day, I had an angina attack; it happened in Paris, one afternoon but I didn't tell anyone. At dusk, I went to the hospital for tests and at ten-thirty the next morning, I was in the office. When I had an angioplasty in New York, two months later, I went into the operating room on a Friday afternoon so I would be ready to get back to work on Monday morning. American doctors understand how you have to fight for your life and they help you to meet the challenge. You feel like a gladiator who has gone down into the arena, which is relatively inhumane. "In Rome", said Cardinal de Retz, "they finish you off when you're down. You'd better not fall!" This is still true, and you have to do everything you can to remain standing. This cruelty by the people who surround you is not, however, a result of spitefulness; it is simply an instinctive reaction. On Wall Street, anyone who runs or has run one of these companies feels a sort of complicity with someone like me: he knows what I am living because he is living it himself. There is a small group of people who do not really know each other but who feel a kind of, not actually compassion – they are incapable of that – but esteem for one another because they are privy to this hyper-competitiveness.

The ideal for Lazard was to have several people with enough stature so that clients would choose to work with one of them. Consequently, it was necessary to select partners who were different but complementary. It was not always easy for partners to get along with each other, precisely because of their diverse characters. I therefore had to form teams made up of very disparate personalities to ensure that friction would be kept to a minimum, since I – and I alone – was responsible for executive decisions.

If I used my influence, it was to allow each person to have some space, which gave the impression of taking away space from anyone who wanted all of it, that is to say, almost all the others. What I did – and this does not happen very often – was to allow different talents to coexist.

This system was very effective for fifteen years, after which it didn't work so well. At first, Lazard's profits increased an amazing fifteen fold between 1977 and 1990. Now it is impossible to continue at that rate, and the impetus slowed down. A bank is like a bicycle: it works as long as you maintain a certain speed but if you go slower, you fall off and crack your head open. But then, once you reach sixty, you have to start considering your successor. As soon as you think about it and try to give more power to one person rather than another, latent jalousies begin to surface. People who were happy working together do not wish to be subordinate to someone who used to be at the same level as them, and so they leave.

That is the sign that it is time to hand over control, which allows the company to head in new directions. However, very often, and this was the case at Lazard, there is no satisfactory successor. An excellent businessman might have no talent whatsoever for running a company. Another person might be capable, but would lack the necessary qualities to assume responsibility for Lazard simultaneously in the United States, France and England. Whatever the case may be, it is impossible to judge the past from the present. You cannot even understand what the situation used to be any longer, and today people claim that my difficulty in finding a successor was due to the fact that I wanted to hold on to control, which was not the case.

Competition between banks has become much fiercer over time because the more established institutions have managed to grow considerably. In 1933, in the United

States, the profession was divided up into investment banks and commercial banks. Consequently, investment banks were kept to a modest size. However, the progressive relaxation of regulations allowed the creation of firms that were far larger. Moreover, when they went public, they were listed on the Stock Market and gave stock options to their executive staff, which made it more attractive to work for them. In a period like 1990 to 2000, when the Stock Market was climbing, companies that paid in shares had an advantage over the others because they provided greater hope of financial gain to their employees than Lazard, for example, who only paid a salary. This happened to such an extent that at the end of this period, many people no longer saw how they could remain with Lazard.

"In the end, a heart either breaks or hardens", as Chamfort put it, and whether we like it or not, with time, the heart does harden a little. The reason why it is impossible to remain in this profession indefinitely is because the affection you feel towards others begins to wane, partly because after having taken a great deal of trouble to help someone's career, you are disappointed when he comes to see you one day and announces: "I feel terrible, but I'm leaving tomorrow". Does this teach you a lesson about the human soul? Not at all. Instead of teaching you something, it takes something away from you. When you are leading a team, the state of innocence you feel when you first begin to mature is preferable because it is combined with affection and enthusiasm. Later on, the enthusiasm remains but the affection diminishes.

CEO/DIRECTOR/HEAD OF LAZARD

I have spent my life trying to reassure people, in spite of themselves, because you don't have to push them very hard before they begin to self-destruct. I have seen people coming out of the office of André Meyer – that great manipulator – beating their breasts, convinced that they alone were guilty in a situation for which they were made responsible. What is strange about human beings is that they are an incredible mixture of a lack of confidence interspersed with spurts of total egotism. They are simultaneously easily convinced that they are in the wrong and equally convinced that their current personal interest is paramount and far more important than the common good. It follows that they are both touching and cruel, torn between a very real desire to have a leader and the equally real desire to take his place. Even the most intelligent people sometimes cannot stay the course because they have a tendency to think only in the short term. And it is true that everything that depends on the economy, and most especially in the investment banking sector, withstands failure with great difficulty, even if it is temporary. What is more, past success is worthless. All that counts is the next deal.

You might have a genuine desire to help people, to motivate them, and this is truly the fragile secret of the kind of collective energy that creates success.

At the same time, the almost desperate cruelty of human beings is rather disconcerting. Very quickly, they brush aside past ties, do not care about the affection you might show them or feelings of gratitude and, in an instant, they are prepared to forget everything in the name of what they consider the life or death need to survive, often hiding their decisions beneath excuses to do with their families. "I have to think of my children", they almost always claim, deluding themselves. It is tempting to reply: "Wait, think about it, are you sure you're not making a mistake?" They look away and betray you.

Things happen at a quicker pace in the business world than in private life. The only difference is that in private life, decisions are harder to make. Consequently, all the destructive tendencies that often remain latent in private life become realities in the business world. In banking circles, the yardstick of success and failure is clear: it is a matter of money and shares. In private life, people use happiness as a benchmark, and that is more vague. In fact, man is a social animal who, more than any other, has the ability to change groups. An elephant does not change group, nor does a gazelle. Man has the capacity of assimilating a great deal of cruelty, because, otherwise, this would be difficult to do. He is prepared to destroy the group he belonged to up until that point. For a long time, I believed that the positive elements of human nature prevailed. Today, however, I find the negative aspects of human behavior equally important. This is undoubtedly linked to the age of the leader of the group... In the animal world, the dominant lion is driven away after he has reigned for two years. We all are capable of experiencing two years of glory, and even ten years in my profession. We were created with a fighting spirit. And then, we pass on the torch.

When young people come to see me because they want to enter the profession, I tell them that they must learn an enormous amount about financial analysis, understanding figures and editing texts. But that has nothing to do with success or failure, which has more to do with a rather classic but mysterious element: having presence. In a certain way, my profession is similar to the theater. Why does an actor who steps on to the stage have presence while another does not? Knowing his job well is not enough, and you can't be taught how to have presence. A young, rather passionate person might give the illusion of presence for a while... People might think: "He has a lot of personality, his own opinions, and he isn't boring." But this might be nothing more than a moment of fleeting grace, due to the vitality of youth, which does count because a large part of presence is a question of energy.

This energy, however, must be backed up by a capacity for sound judgment and authority. All these things evolve. I have always advised people to continually wonder whether they agree or not. Every time you are presented with a matter, ask yourself: "If I were the head banker, what would my attitude be towards this case if I were responsible for it?" Think about it. "If I were the client, what would my attitude be? Would I make a success of this project and, if so, how?" Not all bankers want answers to these questions. They can set out the pros and cons for you...

I am not putting myself forward as an example but when I am presented with a case file, my goal is always to make a decision. Then there is the question of presence. You either have it or you don't – and if you do, it's a gift.

To question yourself, even when you haven't yet made a mistake, seems essential to me. A certain distance and consistency are necessary in order to remain strong and uncompromising because the danger in life is to be damaged by either success or failure or both. In other words, I do not think it is possible to know if you are a good banker before you have experienced some form of failure. Obviously, it is better if the failure is not too serious, otherwise is will finish you off. You must have been able to overcome it even though it has taken the wind out of your sails. I have often said: "That person is a very good man but he still hasn't failed at anything, so we'll have to wait and see." And he will fail; it's inevitable. Character and courage in the face of adversity are extremely important, but considerable flexibility and determination are also essential... To run a bank, you need more determination and less flexibility. This is why it is so difficult to find company leaders. You may spot talent, though this doesn't happen often; but in the end, it is like a great work of art: every now and again, talent is so obvious that you simply can't ignore it.

Teams work best when they are happy. I have always thought that it was necessary to amuse one's colleagues and inspire them with enthusiasm because it is difficult to imagine how very tiresome it is to have to win over every new client you meet. Partners and bankers in general also need to be stimulated. An iconoclastic CEO who mistrusts the accepted truths of the moment can amuse his colleagues while helping them to evolve. The tragedy of professionals today is that they want to set down rules for everything and consequently always cling to accepted judgments. Now, every situation is unique and the role of a CEO is to help his colleagues question themselves. There is a very strong chance that accepted ideas are incorrect. For this reason, analysts work themselves to death trying to predict how much money a company is going to make. To determine its value, they multiply what it earns by a multiple of between six and forty-five, which makes no sense. In order to appear scientific, they calculate the "discounted cash flow", that is, the prediction of how much available cash a company will have in future. They then use this figure to calculate a company's value. Once again, this is a pure convention because they cannot predict how much cash a company will have any more than they can know the discount rate. No scientific procedure is therefore possible. The more a CEO can challenge the confidence of professionals, the more possibility he has of arousing their curiosity, and he then has a chance of prompting them to do some real thinking.

During a phase that has now fortunately passed, at least in part, what took the place of analyzing a company was nothing more than a page of figures that did not even relate to their activities. It drove me crazy! The most important thing in economics, and therefore in the banking profession, comes down to a question of good common sense. It is not actually a very complicated profession, even if it is difficult to carry out, because other parameters, psychological ones to be specific, also come into play.

All economics is based on an extraordinary mixture of rules that are easy to understand and a sequence of events whose consequences are unknown because they are influenced by psychology. Take, for example, the rise of the euro in relation to the dollar, along with its many effects. Is it good or bad for the economy? Most people say: "It's bad, it discourages exports." Someone else says: "It's good, because it makes imports less expensive". The price of oil and natural gas therefore go down, since they are bought in dollars. So this is one positive aspect. People then say: "This is bad for French exports". But which exports? 60% of French exports go to the euro zone, so this only affects exports outside the euro zone, which represents 15% of the economy. Therefore, it is bad for 15% of the economy and either indifferent or good for the other 85%. These are undeniable facts. Now, what can we deduce from these figures? "It's anybody's guess"; no one knows, and that is where the true problem lies. What will be the psychological reactions? Will it discourage or encourage investors? Will a strong currency inspire confidence or not? In reality, given the multiplicity of effects, discerning what will win out is an art that defies analysis.

What is of primary importance in this profession is to know the facts, which is not always easy because people generally present you with only one side of the story. You have to dig a little deeper to discover the hidden facts. But that is not enough: if you have to choose between two companies who have similar products and results, knowing their results, but also their volume of investment is essential. In other words, the real problem is evaluating the significance of the investment. The answer to that question changes everything since one of the two companies will have an advantage, but which one? The one that invests a lot? The one that doesn't invest? It depends. And, in the end, it is intuition more than any other factor that leads you to prefer one to the other... Because it is important to realize that a time will come when everyone will have the same opinion: 90% of people will claim that the company that invests is preferable to another, or *vice versa*, because there is a prevailing atmosphere of what is in fashion that shifts public opinion in a particular direction. If you build a huge factory to manufacture a product that is not yet in demand, it is obviously less prudent than if it produced something already much in demand. The arena is perhaps much more open ended in the first scenario, but the speculative nature of business makes it even more necessary to possess the skills that allow you to interpret the realities of the situation. You must, therefore, first ask yourself if it is worth the trouble.

I always annoyed my partners with one of my beliefs, even though I didn't mention it that often: "From time to time, you have ten bad years". This provocative statement, which runs contrary to the notion of automatic progress, is valuable in emphasizing how much arbitrariness and superficiality exists in the desire for immediate gratification, a desire that has been established as a virtue and sacrosanct. For people who carry out a profession on a day-by-day basis, and particularly in present times, it is heresy to dare to think that you could have "ten bad years" without it being the end of the world.

The fragility of certain institutions comes from the fact that they have great difficulty in surviving brief periods that are relatively worse than others. This is absurd because life is not a permanent ascent. The world can go through poor phases that are relatively long, whether it is a question of the economy, painting or literary activity. But today, there is a religion of constant progress, propped up by an abundant amount of writing and a press that preaches the idea that companies must improve every quarter in a way that is virtually miraculous, regardless of the state of the world. This is what leads to the worst failings and is the primary cause of the excesses and aberrations in management. It has been said so often that it is normal to constantly increase profits that people have done anything and everything, including all of the stupid things. They get carried off on a wave of enthusiasm that is totally unreasonable – extreme speculation for example – to try to avoid poor results.

I ran Lazard in a decentralized way and I think that today, people prefer a more centralized management style. I was successor to André Meyer who had a centralized management style. There is no set recipe; there are just ways of doing things that work for a while… In the business world, you constantly waver between centralized and decentralized management. When I was young, I thought it was an extraordinary waste of time to completely change a company's organization, but today I believe that alternating in this way is a good thing.

It greatly amused me – a word that made André Meyer furious – being able to play a role in the business world, particularly in the United States. "How can you say it's *amusing*! It's interesting, it's our life, it's exciting, yes, but *amusing*?" The distance I kept exasperated him. But yes, it amused me a great deal to be like a boxer who was a champion in France or Europe and who decides to go and make his name in the United States because it is only there that he can be recognized as one of the all-time greats. Amusement does not preclude fear. You must constantly ask yourself if you are in a good enough strategic position so that you have more chance of winning than of losing. It is not really a question of war because there is no opponent other than yourself, but you are still competing. And my sporting analogy is very appropriate: even if there is a difference between a champion who has been amazingly successful and another who has not, any champion's reign must one day end in defeat. And at every moment throughout his career, there is a niggling doubt, and the question is always the same: will *this* be the time I'll be out for the count?

On Travel

Even when work took up most of my time, I always chose to go travelling now and again.

It was my mother who encouraged me to travel when I was still very young. She could tell that I wanted to travel and thought it was an excellent idea. I was barely fifteen years old when I began travelling alone with one of my school friends from Cannes. Our first trip was to Provence and Burgundy. Obviously, we weren't old enough to drive, so the police kept an eye on us because we looked like two little runaways! What's more, we always stayed at the best hotels. We once ran into a friend of my parents in Arles; she was stunned to see two young boys having dinner alone at the Hôtel Jules-César. The following year, we went to Greece, then Spain. When I was eighteen, I went to see Morocco with one of my cousins; the following year, it was Black Africa with another friend. He was half Russian and has since died. He was an inveterate womanizer. His mother prepared his food with specific ingredients, in the recommended amounts, so he would be better at making love, and that was all he could think about.

When we left to visit French Equatorial Africa – Chad, Oubangui-Chari, Central Congo, the Gabon – he embarrassed me by wanting to buy a wife in every village! One night, I woke up feeling someone rather cold beside me: it was a girl he had brought back for me, rather charming actually, who didn't speak a word of French and whose teeth were chiselled and shaped like spikes... At Fort-Archambault, we hired a professional hunter. I later discovered that he had been recommended to me because he had astronomical debts at a local trading post! He was a former officer in the air force who had fought with the Vichy troops in Lebanon against the Free French; he was a horrible drunkard, truly insane. He set fire to the savannah one evening, which is rather dangerous because the wind can quickly change direction. Another time, he wounded a buffalo, an animal known to be aggressive when injured, and he asked us to go and get it. My friend was terrified and rushed up a tree. But I was even more frightened by the idea of having to climb a tree than I was by being attacked by an animal!

There were some extraordinary people in Africa... I remember one evening we spent with a man from Alsace. He lived in a large, rather beautiful hut with no electricity and was fascinated by local magic. When he told those stories on that dark African night, even I, who believe in nothing, must admit that I felt the presence of occult forces. There was also something romantic about this adventure, a feeling of being at the very end of the earth... In the morning, we saw the French flag being raised at Fort-Lamy, in Chad... French Equatorial Africa was quite extraordinary at that time. I remember passing the Djibouti airfield one day at four o'clock in the morning.

All the French military aircrews were getting ready to take off before it got too hot.

There were, however, racist incidents, and they were frequent. One event left me rather puzzled: a white woman, who believed that crocodiles would eat only Blacks, swam across a river to get to the other side and got herself eaten! Another time, I had invited our driver to have lunch with us and the owner of the restaurant asked me if he was a Cabinet member. "These days," he added, "you have to be careful; you can't automatically refuse to serve Blacks; they might be Ministers." There was a certain tension in people's relationships that was very unpleasant. In the French style of colonization, relations with the population were often close, which made it possible to meet people, but sometimes this posed difficulties because sleeping together complicated matters! The English kept their colonists at arm's length, which was totally different from the French attitude.

The English belong to a country of clans. They immediately say: "I'm not English; I'm Scottish or Welsh...." And if someone is English, he states the specific region he comes from, the north or the south-east, etc.

Added to this, there are all the other clannish distinctions that stem from the educational establishments one attended. When transposed to the colonies, such a social structure seemed logical to tribal countries in Africa or in India, where they have a cast system. Since the English were the most powerful, they were considered a dominant tribe or a superior cast, but that did not upset anyone since the natives were not shocked by the concept of a new cast or a different tribe. And everything they did reinforced that idea: their everyday customs, like drinking tea at six o'clock in the morning, getting dressed for dinner, playing specific sports in specific clubs... Just as a Brahman would not wish to mix with an inferior cast, or a member of one tribe would not socialize with someone from another, an Englishman would not mix with the rest of the population. Their attitude was therefore perfectly appropriate and acceptable, and it worked.

When you go to England, you also feel that you come from another tribe. There is no true communication, but no disdain either. There is just the strangeness of being an outsider. French colonization was almost the opposite, and far more generous, because it was a matter of "assimilating the natives" based on the notion that anyone could become French. The English do not think that everyone can become English; they even believe it is totally out of the question.

Everything is interesting when you travel. You have to know how to take your time, savor each moment, not be too demanding. Just because no one has seen a particular monument, you don't necessarily have to rush to visit it. You frequently remember things that seem a waste of time at the moment, but unpleasant experiences often make for wonderful memories.

I love the diversity of different worlds. At the beginning, this love came to me, oddly enough, through music. In my youth, I had a great feel for non-western music: African chants, songs from the North American Indians, Indonesian music, popular Indian music. And this music revealed things that allowed me to get closer to the heart of those civilizations.

What is fascinating about moving around the Earth's surface is seeing that the center of the world has also shifted and that its order has been profoundly shaken, even if I remain the same whether in the Faubourg Saint-Honoré or the savannah. I adapt, of course, because I need to make myself understood. This is necessary and becomes natural but, wherever I am, I always sound very proper, I don't own any sport shoes and I dress in the same way – or nearly!

In central Asia, you notice that you are physically at the center of the world. Not at the ends of the earth, but right at the center, because this is where all cultural influences meet. There are elements that are Indian, Chinese, Greek, Mogul, Islamic... The result is magnificent. In Afghanistan, the fusion of people's features reflects this diversity. One part of the population looks Mogul, another Arab, another Indian and yet another practically European. In the United States, you are at the center of the world, but once in Europe, you have the same feeling. The center of the world is wherever you happen to be! To see the world from India is to understand it differently than if you were in France, the United States or China. In Brazil, I was very surprised to enter into a world of specific cultural references. The Brazilians have two artistic traditions that mean a great deal to them: the Late Baroque of the seventeenth and eighteenth centuries and modern art. Portinari is a painter I had never heard of, yet he is a national hero and collectors are delighted if they own one of his works. Here we find an entire worldview based on national culture. And when you live in Brazil or Iraq, it is truly very far away... A person's view of the world is based on where he comes from, but it is transformed and enriched by what he has experienced while travelling.

For a long time, whenever I arrived in a country I hadn't visited before, I had the habit of going to the movies, preferably to see a film I had already seen. I was immediately plunged into real life, so to speak, with local people going to the same show as me. In Teheran, I recall being in a movie theater where there were only men and where they found the presence of my wife Hélène strange. But in India, I go to the movies because I adore Indian films. I don't mean the Bengali cinema, which is lauded by European intellectuals, but the films made in Bombay and Madras that are popular and extravagant and which today are known as "Bollywood". I find these films tremendously charming. At any moment, a woman will stand up and begin to sing. There is dancing and everything happens in an eternal Spring. You can understand how Kashmir is mythical to Indians, for the good reason that to them, this is where eternal Spring is located, a sort of Paradise in the Indian imagination. And it is difficult for them to give that up. Today, that area has unfortunately become dangerous.

The map of the world is changing. Situations get worse, then improve. In the meantime, there are horrors. But who would have thought that I would one day see peace in Cambodia? Or that I could fly my private plane to Hanoi? Travelling in such conditions is very educational in assessing the state of the planet, even if I am not flying the plane myself. If you go from Paris to Nairobi on an American airline it was impossible to fly over Libya and the Sudan; you have to cut across a bit of Saudi Arabia and the sea. The last time I went to central Asia, we had to take a route over Pakistan to avoid flying over Tibet and Afghanistan.

Whenever I arrive in a new country, I always wish I could get a subscription to a local newspaper and that I could understand the native language. When you read French, English or American newspapers, you do get a wide variety of analyses, but it would be better to add an Indian or Brazilian or Kenyan newspaper... The Africa as seen by a Frenchman, an Englishman or an American is very different. The English and Americans do not realize that western Africa exists. And Tanzania is unimaginable to the French.

Reactions towards modernity, work and progress differ greatly according to where you happen to be. These ideas are often more powerful outside of Europe, but not everywhere. In the Arab world, the notion of progress does not exist as a necessity. Egypt has great difficulty in accepting modern developments and it is not the only country in this situation. The massive influx of people to Cairo caused the city to overflow. On the other hand, India has accepted modernity rather well, even with all the difficulties it has experienced and continues to face. Calcutta was more overcrowded forty years ago than it is today. Rio is on the verge of overflowing, but Bahia is not. Mexico is about to explode: twenty million inhabitants who can't manage to peacefully coexist. Beijing has developed in an astounding and anarchic way, but it's working, more or less. And why? Societies succeed when people believe in the future, because they are working. Otherwise, societies fall to pieces. In Mauritius, where the standard of living is much worse than on Reunion Island, people are relatively satisfied with their existence, because when people have work, they feel that their lives will improve and that creates a very different atmosphere. On Reunion Island, people have contributed little to the future and barely think about it, as if at some time in their history, they came to a fork in the road and chose the wrong path... Countries like the ones that made up ex-Indochina have suffered a great deal, but they never gave up. They threw themselves back into reconstructing, more or less efficiently. It isn't perfect; there is much chaos in these countries because they are not very organized, but they retain the hope that a happy future is possible.

No population is safe from potent acts of horror; this is what the twentieth century has tragically taught us. In the past, people thought that some races were "savages" and others "civilized".

Today, we know that so-called "civilized" peoples can turn into "savages". This happens just as much in Europe as in Asia or Africa. Horror renders everyone equal... we have come to accept the idea that anything can happen anywhere, tomorrow or even today. We live in a world in which the feeling of insecurity is more acute than in the past, and this is rather a new phenomenon. When you read the French newspapers of the 1900s, you can see that even then, people were very afraid of social disorder. There was anarchy and assassination attempts; it wasn't at all peaceful but social foundations were nevertheless

A TASTE FOR HAPPINESS

very well-ordered, at least that was people's impression. At present, everyone senses that anything might explode anywhere, at any time. But you have to admit that this makes travelling even more exciting! I remember the extraordinary atmosphere in Cuba a few months after Fidel Castro took power: a mixture of fervor and collapse, with entire neighborhoods half deserted. When societies find themselves at a turning point in their history, people feel a kind of jubilation that is linked to physical danger and the breakdown of social institutions. Human nature surges forth, for better or for worse. At first, for better, because everyone has realized that in troubled times, people are very kind... until they start killing you.

If I have loved travelling so much, it is primarily because of my love of art. And when you travel, thank heavens, the beautiful things you see do not make you think of the horrors but rather of the happy times.

To me, travelling has symbolized the quest for all possible forms of beauty. Seeking out places where art fills you with joy makes a landscape twice as beautiful. You can rediscover what has long since gone: the ruins of Palmyra, the temples of Angkor, a world that once existed but is no more. It is phenomenal to see how very quickly civilizations come and go. The ones that disappear more slowly are the ones that are not based on physical objects. The Chinese civilization, based on writings, has endured. It is the same for the Jewish civilization. The temple of Jerusalem may have been destroyed but the Bible survived. And so it should be noted that the quest for immortality, which is the basis of all tangible artistic creations, was a failure – often a glorious failure – but a failure nonetheless.

I delight in discovering an art form that is unfamiliar to me. I always wish to discover other sorts of talents, aside from the ones I am familiar with, because, deep down, my heart's desire is to attain a kind of encyclopaedic knowledge. This is why I am interested in Islamic art. It manages to combine two elements that are often contradictory elsewhere: rigor and opulence. Jean David-Weill, my uncle who was a curator at the Louvre, was a great expert in understanding Islamic Art in Damascus, Cairo, Teheran, central Asia and northern India. What I find so enchanting about this art is the severity of its structure in relation to the opulence of its execution. We have illustrations of this in Western Art, stained glass windows for example, but it is inherent in Islamic art. The art of India also fascinates me, although I am less enamored of the Mogul art of the north, which is a type of Muslim art that has been re-worked and modified in keeping with an immense country of considerable wealth. It always makes me want to pull back because I find it suffers terribly from gigantism and because it is inferior to Persian art. On the other hand, the Hindu art of the southern temples with their erotic sculptures – those wonderful female figures with their voluptuous breasts and sinuous bodies – delight me because of the feeling of abundance, exuberance and unbelievable sensuality they manage to convey. Moreover, if a religion exists that I might find tempting, it would have not one god but hundreds of them and would also include women, children, romance... This was the case in the religion of Ancient Greece, and it is also true of India.

Many gods exist to Indians and you find yourself in a very warm and convincing universe. Here is life, and contradictions. Everything is made of contrasts: the same god can be good or evil. I find that enchanting! A bit further away towards the East, the Chinese Buddhist statues are absolutely wonderfully meditative, glowing with grace from within. And they owe much to India, even though they are completely Chinese.

The world of boundaries pleases me enormously because they represent the fusion of two civilizations expressed in a major art form. I love the Hindu side of China, the Arab-Berber art of Andalusia, the Greek side of Afghanistan. I am moved by the civilization of the Late Middle Ages and by Carolingian art where Romanesque, Byzantine, Merovingian and even Barbarian influences can be felt all at once... All these evolutions result from a complex interaction of influences and are very important.

A painter like Antonello of Messina was probably the first European painter. Although from Messina, as his name indicates, he was greatly influenced by northern Europe – and he was a major artist. It is the same for the birth of French Art in the seventeenth century: it was the fruit of all sorts of developments in the way that beauty could be expressed, with a common ideal but slightly different ways of proceeding, similar enough for us to be able to recognize ourselves and yet different enough for it to always remain a precious discovery of something new.

Nothing compares to seeing things in their own environment because they are surrounded by their unique light and spiritual force. In Delphi, one can feel the gods. Above Jerusalem, there is almost a kind of cloak that encloses a network of different religions within the city. At the Mosque in southern Jerusalem, you find yourself amid the majesty of the Muslim world. Yet, a few meters away, at the Wailing Wall, you have the intense impression that you are in the presence of the echoes of Jewish prayers going back thousands of years. The Christian world is represented in its diversity (with the exception of the Protestants) at the Holy Sepulchre; it is a wonderful place. You can almost palpably feel the harmonious chanting of prayers to heaven. Simply walking into the cathedral at Chartres is in itself a religious experience. I remember the ornamental paving stones at its entrance: you feel as if you are walking into a French farm. It is this simplicity which I find so moving and which is its gift: the art of making something which you can no longer do without once you have seen it because it is natural and therefore necessary, like a familiar landscape. I have the same feeling when standing before Romanesque churches which seem to rise out of the earth, while in Italy, I often have the impression that they are a bit designed to impress, with their somewhat flashy façades. And then there is Benares... I greatly shocked a gentleman who worked for Lazard in India because when he asked me: "What are you going to do over the week-end?" I replied: "I am going to Benares." He was horrified, because to an Indian like him, it was an old-fashioned spot that did not reflect his modern aspirations in any way. It is a place where you are completely gripped by faith, tangible at every moment in people's attitude, in the rites linked to life and death, in its majestic river. The beauty of the world seen from the Ganges at sunrise and sunset is full of subtlety and is such a splendid sight that it is impossible not to be transfixed...

India has influenced me deeply. You immediately feel you are arriving in another world, a world with different values. This was the impression I had during my first visit there in 1955, and it has been the same ever since. The Western way of life has had such success all over the world that when you find yourself in a place where everything is completely different, it is very surprising. The dead can be seen on the streets, being transported on a palanquin to the crematoriums, which are in full sight. All these things have contributed to my belief that death is a normal part of life, something we shouldn't fear because it is everyone's destiny and so it is better not to get so upset about it. This idea already existed in my family, but in India, I was able to get close to an entire race of people who shared it.

This natural relationship to death was the greatest revelation to me, with the simultaneous discovery of the fantastic visual beauty of India in all its various forms: the charm of its people, their innate elegance, their sophistication that does not rely on financial means (as Naipaul very ably describes in his stories about Brahman families living well below the poverty line), as well as the ability that Indians have to adapt to change while continuing to be individuals, even in a crowd. Traces of the British Empire were still obvious in the 1950s... The hotels were imposing buildings with verandas all the way around. I remember nights of scorching heat when the beds were taken out onto the lawns and the clients slept beneath the beautiful stars under mosquito nets. I also remember the old English clubs in the small towns where the newspapers were three months old and people welcomed you by serving tea...

Later on, I discovered the joy of the countryside in Africa and the United States. It is impressive. Everywhere else, people believe they are far more important and have a greater place than they really do in relation to the universe. In a great expanse of land, we are reduced to our proper size. It is a rather exceptional experience to suddenly become aware of man's finiteness compared to the immensity of the world. Added to that, in Africa, we experience the revelation that we are not the only inhabitants of the planet. I never tire of watching the animals that live in the wild.

That spectacle teaches so many things and I never cease feeling astounded by how very much it helps me to understand the people around me more and more! And to a feminist like me, it is a lesson in male chauvinism. The dominant male stays for a few seasons, at most, and all social organization depends on the female world – in elephants, monkeys and lions. But at the same time, there is the primacy of the male, which serves no purpose. Indisputably, he dominates because of his aggression and physical beauty. And so there exists a hierarchy based on certain attributes. First, there is aggression, followed by tactics, then mutual aid, then all other power relationships. Animals adapt to their surroundings. In France, there is no doubt that members of the deer family prefer prairies to forests, but they live in the forest because they can no longer live on the prairies. When a herd of elephants arrives in a region where they are not welcomed by the local population, their nervousness and behavior is very characteristic of anxiety, but they calm down after a few days when they are in a spot where they are accepted. Panthers can wander about in the middle of crowds in a city without much difficulty, which is actually rather dangerous.

If the discovery of nature is relatively recent in my life, it is not because I did not love nature. I actually love French nature a lot, because it provides a wonderful feeling of certainty that everything has been transformed by man. In Quercy, the Rouergue or the Dordogne regions, the landscape has been constantly altered over forty thousand years; even when there is a feeling that an area has been untouched, it has been landscaped by man. Along with the almost incomprehensible miracle that the buildings are in keeping with the surroundings. I remember passing through a village in the Île-de-France region not long ago, where there were two ancient buildings beside a pond. They did not stand out particularly and I thought: "It is incredible that these buildings were not constructed with any kind of aesthetic in mind and yet they are beautiful." And by chance! The same chance that made France or Italy... And why? Because they are in harmony with their surroundings. There is, doubtlessly, a sense of taste that runs deeper than learned taste because it is virtually instinctive and the sign of true civilizations.

When I see how Las Vegas casinos have been designed, I am truly baffled. Would they be better if they were not so garish? Not necessarily... One day, I heard some people say: *"They take our money but they treat us right."* Such excessive popular extravagance has replaced the ersatz luxury of casinos of the past, where a certain notion of sumptuousness was aimed at the middle classes who were impressed by such opulence, rather than at the working classes, who might be dazzled by the décor, but who would never have dreamt of living in such splendor.

Many places have been ruined: the Spanish coast, one of the former capitals of Thailand to the north of Bangkok, the French suburbs and, even more so, the suburbs of many cities in the United States. But the French Riviera has not been spoiled because, thanks to a kind of disorder, it has more or less managed to retain its charm. When things are too well-ordered, it's worse, and this is the case on the coasts of Spain where twelve storey buildings are being constructed, one after the other, stretching over a hundred kilometers, and where nature is being destroyed on a massive scale. This is irreparable, while elsewhere, the landscape manages to absorb a hodge-podge of buildings that are springing up here and there.

Fortunately, it is often only necessary to travel a few kilometers in any direction to discover some wonderful areas. Certain places improve with time. When I first went to Tokyo, I found the city terrible, but the last time I was there, I thought it was rather beautiful. American cities have made fantastic progress after going through a period of total dilapidation in the 1950s and 60s. They have improved today, even if there are incongruities, like skyscrapers in the middle of nowhere. When you arrive in Dallas, which sits in the middle of vast plains, and see its high towers, you wonder what they are doing there. It's not ugly; it even has something of the "Tower of Babel" about it that I like. In the United States, where nature is very present because the country is so immense, such a defiant gesture makes sense. Americans must assert themselves in the face of those phenomenal open spaces, and this gigantism, which at first sight seems incomprehensible, soon becomes attractive. The artificial dimensions of these constructions may make the architecture less beautiful than what would seem more naturally suitable, but it can also be very successful.

The presence of skyscrapers in New York is understandable; the island of Manhattan is not very big and is built on rock. But I never liked the Twin Towers; I found them inelegant. You can't build something 380 meters high that is not imposing, but no one ever tried to integrate them into their environment: it was awful. It was just essential that they could be seen from everywhere. It is perhaps sacrilegious to say this after what happened to them. Nevertheless, I would not have enjoyed having an office there. On the other hand, some other buildings in New York are very beautiful, with very clean lines. They have a personality, which is rather a mystery. Take Rockefeller Center, where I have the great pleasure of having my office, or the Chrysler Building, built in the 1930s, or the Flatiron Building that dates from the 1910s, an era when many buildings constructed in New York were based on the austere architecture of Florence. This is why I used to say: "Why go to Florence when you can go to Wall Street?" Florence is a sad city, very forbidding; its cathedral is awful, conceived like some big wedding cake with gaudy colored icing. And what's more, it is a city of old-fashioned bankers! Wall Street is better. In New York, for example, the Federal Reserve Building was built on the model of the palaces in Florence: it is a gloomy building but a bit grander and therefore better. What made me change my mind about Florence was the painting that came from there: it is incredible... and the Early Italian Renaissance is one of the periods I love the most in all of the world.

What first shocked me in Italy was the fact that the country looked as if it were not well-kept, but that has since improved. For someone who does not like disorder – chaotic traffic, terrible noise everywhere, ruins – it was a scene from hell! To many people, that is part of Italy's charm, just like the empty palaces and crumbling ruins... But they do nothing for me, especially since I take no pleasure in seeing people who are more or less delighted by their decadence. To make things even worse, I do not like Italian food. Since they put grated cheese on everything, I always have the feeling I'm eating soap! And the further south you go, the more you are served things swimming in black ink, not to mention all the slimy animals they try to get you to eat... And tomato sauce and olive oil on everything are supposed to make it better! The worst of all is that little ball of rubber that pretends it's a cheese: mozzarella. It's like eating a white tire! Around the Piedmont area the food is better, but the wine is undrinkable anywhere, north or south.

At the risk of damning myself for good, I must admit there is another type of food I find terrible: Japanese. Those slices of raw red fish are one of the most disgusting things I have ever seen! Plus all that seaweed and little cubes of tofu... And the clear soup that starts all their meals and reminds me of the medicine I took as a child. In order for a medicine to be effective, it had to taste bad, and it is the same with Japanese soup. People are in heaven seeing meat cooked right before their eyes, but that goes back to Caveman times! I can remember a gala dinner in Tokyo where not one of the forty dishes served was edible! There are only two acceptable types of food: French and Chinese, with one exception – and this will be even more shocking than the two types of cooking I have said I dislike – and that is the American sandwich. They are very well made with just the right amount of mayonnaise and lettuce and a successful contrast between what is soft and what is crunchy.

I have the joy of belonging to the *Club des cent*, a gourmet society where members meet for lunch in Paris. It is a very special, sophisticated place where people are extremely pleasant to one another. They come from the most diverse backgrounds: businessmen, doctors, lawyers... and you meet some amazing people there. And while I am hardly fond of clubs in general, I have been delighted to meet these men – there are only men – who are very warm, very friendly, very cultured, who are knowledgeable about both food and farming regions, and therefore know where products come from, where to find them and the best times of year to get them. To have good taste and recognize quality are truly the signs of a great civilization. Nevertheless, I have ceased doing battle with many of my dislikes. And so, I go boating, even though I continue to believe that only the coastlines are interesting and... I even go to Italy.

But there is so much that makes up Italy... Since it is a country that is fairly new in terms of history, created from independent principalities, there is little relationship between Turin and Milan, Rome, Naples and Florence; each has a personality that endures. I find Rome boring;

Roman antiquities are deadly dull. The Vatican Museum is not well-organized, stuffy, gloomy to visit and stifling. I do admire the Villa Medici, the gardens, the Farnese Palace... Naples is enjoyable, but it is not beautiful in the way I like: too Baroque for my taste. I have the impression that there is a kind of mockery of art, even though it is actually rather beautiful... Artists from Naples hide behind a tradition of irony; they like overdoing everything. Faced with the poverty and the glory that is all around them, this is perhaps a very good reaction, but it remains quite foreign to me.

I like Sicily, where Greece and the Muslim world co-exist. Palermo is full of churches with Arabic symbols whose columns come from ancient sites. This mixture of two great civilizations, along with a kind of severity on people's faces and in the landscape – both very abrasive – make it a magnificent country. And I like Venice (which I do not consider to be Italian); its disorganized accumulation of so many talents and buildings delights me. I wouldn't live there because it is impossible to ignore the fact that it is a city of commerce whose trade has vanished. In Venice, one witnesses the spectacle of a world of merchants that once existed, but, even more, a world that formed their psyches and was the very spice of their lives. They were not aesthetes, rather men who enjoyed action and pleasure. I managed to visit the women's casino that today belongs to the French Cultural Service. It is a rather small place where people enjoy conversation and gambling and where only women used to be allowed. It must have been divine... But Venice remains magical and is the only place where it is thoroughly enjoyable to get lost because it is very safe. In addition, you only have to walk a few steps in any direction to see a dazzling sight. I go there to spend a few days at a hotel. I never see anyone. If you want to disappear, it is easy to hide there... There are certain areas where people can go for a walk in perfect tranquillity, far away from everything. And I am delighted by the Doge's Palace because it symbolizes the very height of achievement.

I love the idea that the paths of civilization can intersect with the paths of trade. There is no art without prosperity. The Italy of the Renaissance was a period of wealth, as was Holland in the seventeenth century. Art can survive adversity; a country can go into decline and still produce works of art, but if prosperity does not return, art withers then dies. In this domain as well, we need to keep hope in the future.

I have always admired those rare individuals who only think about the present. I am sure that it is possible to experience pure pleasure many times a day. However, except for a few admirable people who are capable of artistic or religious meditation, only the desire for what is to come in the future provides the impetus for appreciating the present. It is not necessary to believe in the future, but it is vital to look forward to tomorrow. I know how to live in the moment quite well, but it is true that my curiosity about the world is more relevant than the future.

In many places, the concept of the "old" and the "new" vanishes. This is why I have come to realize that certain areas that seem as if they have great natural beauty are actually new, like the luxuriant forests all around Rio that replaced the former coffee plantations after 1910. The Japanese reconstructed temples identical to ancient ones, which is why their ninth century temples were built five years ago. All the palaces in St. Petersburg were destroyed during the Second World War, so they are all new. And to tell the truth, I don't like them very much because I find them extraordinarily similar, each with the same enormous gold and white reception room. The lack of novelty in these buildings saddens me, and the fact that this is intentional is not convincing.

It also upsets me greatly to see that my contemporaries like desolate landscapes. By seeking out isolation, they construct a false solitude. Because they have to be able to come and go relatively easily, they prefer dried up hills to fertile valleys, swampland to coffee plantations, snow-covered peaks to villages... All my life, I have disputed the validity of theories expounded by western tourists who believe that the inhospitable countryside is more attractive than fertile land. I am wary of the extreme landscapes that are in fashion and I like harmony between nature and civilization.

I am always happy to arrive in populated places. I shock people in Africa: I am delighted by the animals, the savannah, etc., but when I catch sight of somewhere with human life, coffee or tea plantations, I breathe rather more easily because I believe in a land of plenty. I am not an enthusiastic fan of asceticism. Moreover, even within asceticism, the thing that is admired in Cistercian Abbeys is that in the middle of their desert world, they have created a place where they can live. It is life that people love, not the desert. At least, that's how it seems to me... In Arab civilizations, the desert is hostile. I hate the Dead Sea, the Syrian Desert; such places are far less interesting than the fertile areas around Damas, California or the Beauce. Yet strangely, many people today only feel at ease in places that are deserted. But they are deserted precisely because no one ever goes there – and no one ever should!

People want to escape from crowds. I can understand this, though I have personally always liked crowds, undoubtedly because I have never had to live in them permanently. From time to time, they can be somewhat overwhelming. I recall visiting Shanghai on a national holiday. There must have been millions of people on the streets; it was impossible to move. The density of Asian populations is quite incredible, but it is accompanied by the very civilized art by which people take up as little space as possible, even if Hong Kong today resembles a New York without people strolling about, and where the efficiency of the modern world is amplified by incomparable harshness. In China, the Cultural Revolution caused the death of people's souls. Fifteen years ago, I felt as if I were visiting a displaced persons' site for people who had just been released from concentration camps. The Chinese bore the scars of their own destruction. No one was innocent any more. They had been immersed in collective horror from which they emerged almost hopelessly driven. The only people who seemed to enjoy living were the elderly: they had a reprieve. For everyone else, it was a merciless struggle and the demonstration of unparalleled materialism. The struggle has continued ever since; it has even become more fierce. The kind of competition that the Chinese engage in is so aggressive that it will soon make today's American Capitalists seem like sweet dreamers.

ON TRAVEL

Wherever I might be in the world, only the Mediterranean gives me the impression that I have come home. And I have always been passionate about Greek art. Nothing else gives me so much joy... There is no self-pride and no defiance in Greek civilization, no Tower of Babel either, just harmony in everything. I feel a connection to Greece. The simplicity of its architecture, the power of its light and the severity of its white hills remind me of Provence, which I so love. All of this with a unique touch of elegance that permeates everything.

Other Worlds

Sleeping is a sensual pleasure. I have sometimes slept for thirteen or fourteen hours in a row between Friday night and Saturday morning. That was quite a while ago; I have been a good sleeper for a long time. Even today, if I am worried about something, I force myself to go to sleep. I virtually succeed in forgetting about a problem until the next day through a conscious effort of blocking it out. I seem to retreat; it goes away, but in reality, by working it through during the night, when I wake up, I find a solution, and this works for every aspect of my life. However, because of the time difference between New York and Paris, which I have regularly experienced for many years, my ability to sleep has become quite disrupted. Rather than complain about it, I decided to turn it into an advantage. I have been very happy to be able to read, all night long on occasion, and to learn, because late-night television programs on both sides of the Atlantic are incredible.

There was even a time when I forced myself to go out, no matter what time it was. Since I normally woke up around three thirty in the morning after returning to Paris,

I would go for a drive in the car. This is rather enjoyable in summer, but less so in winter because it is cold and you feel drowsy, even if it is still entertaining and sometimes even poignant. At the end of the Boulevard Saint-Michel, there was one café that closed at five o'clock in the morning and another that opened at the same time. You could almost carry your cup of coffee from one to the other. And they each had a group of people who were either already there or had just arrived, in the space of a minute. Some of them were people who hadn't gone to bed and, quite often, unfortunate couples who didn't know where to go at four thirty in the morning. Others were people who were bravely going to work, people you could sense would be invisible all day long, and because they were the first and only ones up at that hour, this was their moment to live their lives.

I have always enjoyed setting aside some time for myself and my greatest desire is not to allow myself to be overcome by the problems of the moment. This means acting quickly but with a certain amount of concentration and not doing more than what is strictly necessary. Even when business matters took up an enormous part of my life, I managed to set aside at least one hour a day for artistic activities, which have always been my passion, and at the week-end, to indulge in the pleasures of life, interrupted from time to time by telephone calls. My method consists of keeping up to date, because there is no other way to be free. If you have fulfilled all your obligations, made all your telephone calls, read all your paperwork, then you are free! To put it another way, you can live life at different speeds and then shift into high gear to be free. And you maintain this equilibrium by safeguarding those moments when you have nothing left to do.

Being privileged enough not to be interested in any sport, I was able to free up a lot of time. If I played golf or watched football games, that would not have been possible. When I feel like going for a walk, I do, but I don't make it a rule; if it's cold or raining, I don't go out. I often find walking boring, though strolling through a museum is never tiring or dull.

The only thing I find exhausting is hearing other people go on and on about their problems. By this I mean someone who talks about his troubles in the same way a dozen times, and it doesn't matter if it is a close friend or a relative. Misunderstandings exasperate me more than anything, to such an extent that I can't even read a book or watch a movie that involves a misunderstanding. Whenever I have the feeling that an author has gone wrong, which happens rather often, unfortunately, I stop reading. And if I willingly offer too many explanations during a conversation, it is first and foremost because I am afraid I might be ambiguous. This is somewhat pointless because too many people have a tendency not to believe you. You are suspected of Machiavellism and that causes great damage. "You can explain things to people," André Meyer used to say, "but you can't understand for them!" And he was right. If they have a complicated plan in mind, they won't understand you; they'll think that what you are saying isn't true, or that you aren't saying exactly what you mean, and a misunderstanding results. Some people cannot help themselves automatically accusing others of false reasoning because they themselves are illogical; they are very intelligent idiots who use twisted logic. Since I believed in the power of logic, it has taken me a long time to realize that you cannot help anyone, so I wasted a considerable amount of energy. It is so rare to be able to convince someone else of the validity of what you think that it is tempting to tell yourself: "If he has understood, he'll change his mind"; but then, in the long run, it changes nothing. There is a bit of irrationality in all people's reactions and no one is completely straightforward. However, the most unbearable of all misunderstandings have to do with feelings: this happens with people who love each other but who don't say so, children who think their parents hate them when they love them very much, people who think someone or other is out to cheat them when they actually only wish them well.

I am the opposite of a betting man *par excellence*... so much so that I kept the Lazard Bank well away from any kind of speculation to a degree that was actually excessive. I judged the most likely pros and cons of every type of decision, whether professional or personal. To make up for it, I like gambling. I feel I am escaping to another world. I find it entertaining to occasionally spend a few hours pitting myself against chance and seeing if it is possible to defy the logical laws of statistics. Given the fact that I am knowledgeable about such laws, I know very well that you always lose in the end. I have often heard about people who lost everything by gambling but I've never seen anyone make their fortune that way. Consequently, my activities in this area have always been cautious and minor. But I do enjoy it!

A TASTE FOR HAPPINESS

Every time I find myself in a city with a casino, I go. And whether it is in Macao, Las Vegas, Monte-Carlo or elsewhere, time seems to fly by. I have sometimes even dragged my family along. I remember one night when my wife Hélène ended up falling asleep with her head on the green felt of a gaming table...

Spending two hours at a slot machine is very relaxing for someone like me because I feel completely free of responsibilities. I recall one day at the casino in Antibes when I won a fantastic amount... As I was getting ready to leave, I saw a group of sinister looking muscle men waiting for me and I thought they were going to beat me up. Far from it! They formed a guard of honor and started applauding.

I have really enjoyed playing poker, which is not a game of luck, because over six hours of playing, the players are ranked according to how well they play the game, and the best man wins. It is a matter of making the most of one's own strengths and exploiting the weaknesses of the others, something that requires keeping cool, the ability to think ahead and a certain toughness. True gamblers are very familiar with the odds; they more or less know what the other players have in their hands and whether they are bluffing. Poker is a game of concealment where psychological interactions are important; it is also a very entertaining and intelligent game that, unlike chess, requires quick thinking. And since I am better at making quick decisions, I prefer poker. But I lack the killer instinct.

I'm not bad at the defensive part of the game because it requires thought, but I hold back when I know I'm going to win. I don't bet enough and don't want to take advantage. What's more, I've never played with people who bet large sums. And I've never played poker in the United States, as I have no desire to create problems with people with whom I do business. I taught my daughters how to play poker, but we only play for nominal amounts. All in all, I am a good player – and an excellent loser as well!

Silence is a necessity. One of my prejudices is thinking that music preoccupies the mind too much because it is an art that requires time. I simply don't like music. Music lovers say that it is greatly relaxing: they empty their minds and are engaged for a relatively long time with something outside themselves. Deep down, I have always thought, whether consciously or unconsciously, that the time spent listening to music would prevent me from reaching the many decisions I had to make every day. On the other hand, far from the frenzy of the world, the moments of silence with no apparent purpose that I have sought to cultivate, even if they are brief, allow me to suddenly find the solution to a problem by letting my unconscious do its work.

The fundamental is often hidden. Beneath an obvious truth there is always another truth that cannot be seen. If you do not look beneath the surface because there isn't enough time, you will draw the wrong conclusion. Most people spend their lives sorting out the problems they encounter along the way, but they forget what is essential. However, this requires more than just an immediate reaction: it takes thought and therefore concentration. This is a relatively mysterious phenomenon because you can't sit down at your desk and tell yourself: "I'm going to take an hour to think about it." You might have to think about it for an hour and then spend twenty minutes in silence, with an open mind, so that, two days later, the answer to the question at hand appears clear to you. I have always wanted to find *the* solution, that is to say, I don't like vagueness. A momentary lack of clarity over details doesn't bother me, but everything must end up as part of a coherent plan.

If I escaped by listening to music, I would lose precious time while my mind wandered. When I look at a painting that I love, I deepen my relationship with the world and do not have the impression that I am removing myself from it. Perhaps because the world of music is foreign to me, I have the feeling that I am going away – or even worse – that I am being pulled out of my world to be thrown into a universe that is not my own. And deep down, it bores me. After ten minutes, I wonder: "What on earth am I doing?" I want to be alone, and not with Mr. Beethoven! In a museum, on the other hand, you are in control of your time. And there is a great difference in tempo: a long visit to a museum is a bit shorter than a symphony. In addition, the composer imposes the length of a piece of music on me. To put it another way, instead of doing what I want, I am dependent on someone else.

The discipline required by a certain submission to the rhythm of the music does not suit me because you have to let yourself be carried away with it. Now, since I hate drugs and dislike the feeling you get from drinking too much, I refuse to allow myself to be under the influence, music included! When I look at a painting or a landscape,

I can do it in thirty seconds, two minutes or much longer if I wish, and having that kind of freedom is gratifying.

Looking at something is never a waste of time. When you live in a city, you have a need that is almost physical to look out at a horizon because it is precisely the feeling of openness that is missing in a city. The ability to regularly cast your eyes far into the distance is good for you. Hence the appeal of the sea... It is extraordinarily relaxing for the eyes, and thus for the spirit, just like looking at the countryside, which corresponds to the idea of field perception in visual perspective. And I also love looking at the sky... There are some fantastic skies. I do not know the stars well – my brother Jean was so impassioned by them – but I get surprising satisfaction from musing at the unimaginable distances that separate the galaxies from our little life here on earth. Every time I am on an airplane, I think of the amazing fact that ten kilometers from the ground, life is no longer possible. The lunar landscape does not particularly appeal to me, but if one day there is a good hotel there, why not go and stay? But not before. I am aware of the shape I am in and, frankly, it would be rather ridiculous! What I find especially fascinating is the series of contingencies that make our world what it is, and, quite by chance, so beautiful.

And the fact that everything exists, against all the odds, seems yet another reason to be happy.

These days, the real world is a luxury. The real world is a tree, but you have to have room to plant it. The real world is grass and the sea. No one can steal the sky from you and it doesn't look the same in New York as it does in the countryside. Knowing someone, having friends, living an adventurous life, are also great luxuries because these things require time, space, a place where people can meet, all real requirements that are not so easy to meet in contemporary society. Consequently, we are living more and more in a world where the virtual prevails. This is a change that deeply alters our habits and who we are.

Anything can be virtual: appearances, human relations, sexuality – you can now take risks with sex without really taking them. Even art can be virtual because you can be provided with a plan of something that might be a work of art if it existed, and it is presented as such. This is one of the newest and most fascinating aspects of today's world. Such a transformation of life is in keeping with urbanization and probably a consequence of it. When people find themselves in such close quarters, it is impossible to move. In ten years, 75% of the African population will be living in cities and sprawling towns are already springing up everywhere. In Paris, we have the advantage of still living in a village, but Mexico, with its twenty million inhabitants, San Paulo and Shanghai are enormous metropolises that require a different type of human interaction. Reality is becoming too restricted, and, consequently, we are moving towards a virtual world, one in which another kind of freedom exists, but that too is virtual. From that point of view, it is a great benefit, a relief, but one that has no basis whatsoever in reality: you are in another world. At your computer, you can re-create vast magical spaces, but they are virtual. You can go wherever you like, see whomever you please, speak to anyone anywhere in the whole wide world... but virtually.

OTHER WORLDS

This is another dimension of the universe and this fact neither shocks nor upsets me, but it is currently beginning to replace what is real. This is also starting to happen in business. Numbers have stopped being real; they are so astronomical that it is becoming difficult to make sense of them. Moreover, the values themselves and the price of things are becoming more and more virtual because they are judged by their future value and their scarcity, and less on their returns or actual value. In economics, the virtual has not yet won out because there's no getting away from the facts, but it is gaining ground.

Certain museums have also begun leaning towards the virtual. Now, as long as art remains an interpretation of reality, I will appreciate it, admire it and it will move me. It might be a question of a very distorted or partial reality, but I find that in no way shocking. However, when that ceases to be true, I am no longer in my element. As long as I can still link Mondrian's drawings to calligraphy, I will be interested in them, even if they are actually a false type of calligraphy... But there is a tendency today to make everything virtual. This is why the works of Impressionist painters that are generally intended for intimate spaces are currently hanging on the walls of the Orsay Museum in enormous rooms that are totally white, in other words, in a quasi-virtual environment, where they can no longer be enjoyed visually but are only able to exist through the message they convey. Fortunately, this method of displaying works of art is today being reversed: the new museum in Vienna is not designed that way at all. And in London, I saw an El Greco exhibition I had visited in New York when it was first being hung; they were paying a great deal of attention to the color of the walls behind the paintings, to properly integrate them into their surroundings. So people are taking more care over the surroundings in which a work of art is placed than they did a few years ago. And this is the least they can do because we must hope that at least the museums will remain firmly fixed in the real world.

On Money

Many people think that money is the driving force in life, others say that it is sex... In my opinion, it is neither. The driving force in life is the thirst for blood. Human beings enjoy killing. They like the act of killing even more than its ultimate result, which is death... I would go so far as to say that even though people might regret killing, they still enjoy it! It is significant that kings and dictators and everyone else who has killed are not badly thought of, quite the contrary... while thieves are always held in poor esteem. So claiming that money is the driving force in life seems inaccurate to me. The major goal and supreme joy is killing – money is only the means by which to do it. The President of the Republic, who is also Commander in Chief, has his finger on the button of the nuclear bomb and it is the fact that he can kill enormous numbers of people that makes his authority more legitimate. We live in a culture of murder. For that reason, we cannot be at peace!

A TASTE FOR HAPPINESS

I have lived my life during a rare, peaceful moment in History, just like the people in the eighteenth century who managed to enjoy a miraculous truce...

In between two periods of conflict, people build cities, palaces, monuments. They grow wealthy and believe in their tangible progress, but that only happens during times of respite. The truly important periods in History are the bloody times when nothing counts but violence or resistance to that violence. At such times, everything is swept away by war, which is the great divider of History. There are the good and the bad, your side and the other side, and everyone claims that God is with him. There are some backward-looking people who believe that it is dangerous to allow foreigners to own the means of production in your own country, but nine times out of ten, this is a complete illusion. Economic war does not exist. As long as businesses are multinational, they can no longer be defined in national terms and therefore represent no threat.

We have been living through one of mankind's propitious but atypical moments of peace and, for my children's sake, I hope it will continue for a while. But I fear I am correct in saying that war is the dominant condition. Violent countries triumph over the non-violent ones, and it is always tempting for the older, prosperous countries to believe the contrary. It is not always the most powerless people who turn to terrorism; it is often those who would normally become peaceful members of the bourgeoisie. It is their taste for blood that attracts them to terrorism because, unconsciously, there is more glory in risking or even sacrificing one's life than in becoming a lawyer, an engineer or a businessman. And, of course, they are young and men rather than women, though there are a few female kamikazes, but they remain the exception.

China is aging at a dizzying pace; all of Europe is aging, and so is Japan. The United States is not, thanks to its considerable number of immigrants, nor is India. The Middle East and Africa are being rejuvenated. Simply by stating these facts, you can draw a map of where the most violence exists, it's as simple as that.

As far as sex is concerned, it is undoubtedly the greatest, most passionate pleasure in life, partly because you can never really entirely understand the other person. Unfortunately, people rarely acknowledge sex as one of the moving forces of their lives. While love remains the greatest preoccupation of both men and women, even if they deny it, their hearts do not really dictate their behaviour.

Very early on, I wondered why my profession was so well paid. There is clearly something unfair about it – I wouldn't go so far as to call it unjust – but it is totally unfair because there are distinguished professionals, doctors for example, who are relatively badly paid, not to mention teachers and museum curators. It isn't fair, but that's how it is. The only justification I can find is that bankers live in a dangerous world where a great deal of money changes hands. Competition in this world is cutthroat and you have to work tirelessly while always remaining alert. Perhaps that deserves being rewarded, to a certain extent. However, I firmly believe that if bankers were not so well paid, society would not necessarily improve.

In any case, it is very difficult to find an efficient way of remunerating company managers.

Stock options, this kind of false democracy in business, troubles me somewhat because, given the nature of investors and the necessity of those institutional investors to get results very quickly, I am not sure that such a sense of urgency is always in keeping with an effective strategy for generating profits in the long term. Sometimes a takeover bid is nothing more than the desire of a group of shareholders to make money quickly. It nevertheless remains true that very few people are capable of managing a business. Companies fight for those people and they are worth a lot of money, just as other talented people are in today's world: a football player, a singer and the president of a company are all very expensive... If you don't want to pay for them, well, then you can't have them! And it is true that our modern world is constructed in such a way that there is a correlation between inequality in salaries and economic growth, which may be frowned upon, but is nonetheless a reality. However, you can have inequality in salaries and still have a society that does not work well, but I do not believe there have been cases of economic growth without inequality in salaries, nor increases in salaries without inequalities. Unfortunately, you can have cases of inequality in salaries without growth, which has often happened in South America, for example. You can choose to have neither, but you cannot have one without the other. It depends on the goals of society. In France, it is currently difficult to assert that competition, globalization, lack of security or, more precisely, the need for change, are essential, which is the truth, because people have been saying the opposite for the past thirty years!

Narrow-mindedness about money and the excessive love of money on the part of those who are already rich are often characteristic of people who don't know how to make money. By definition, those people are very attached to wealth because, to them, it is a question of fact – you either have money or you don't – and, in addition, it is an unstable condition. People either want more money in order to have the upper hand over others and to acquire a certain social standing through wealth, or they are intoxicated by having money to burn and the idea of possessing an abundance of material riches which allows them to burst forth like so many fireworks. To me, as well as to most people who carry out the same type of work as mine, money simply moves: it comes and it goes...

I could describe myself as French, Catholic, Jewish, living abroad, loving the United States, but the characteristic that others would probably think of first – great wealth – isn't really a characteristic at all. Instead, I consider it the result of work, with the idea, however, that if I do less work, I will have less money at my disposal... In short, wealth is not an intrinsic part of who I am.

Where money is concerned, I have never felt any guilt whatsoever, nor any pride, for that matter... Probably because it seems all too natural to me. Given two pieces of fabric which would be identical to 99% of the population, one of them hand-embroidered and the other machine-made – one costing ten times the other and, honestly, only 10% better in quality – I would not hesitate for a moment: I would choose the one that was ten times more expensive because I considered it better. Whenever anyone talks to me about economizing, I feel uncomfortable. And when you have eclectic taste, as I do, the opportunities to spend all your money are absolutely incredible! I have just acquired the most exquisite pair of seventeenth century Chinese vases with French eighteenth century gilt-bronze mounts. And it is a joy to go home in the evening and look at them. It would take me no time at all to make a list of ten works of art that I would love to own but which are beyond my means. I prefer a very good restaurant to a very bad one; I normally travel in first class rather than in economy, but I do not think it is essential. In addition, I do not wish to do it all the time, and even less so if it seems it is for the sake of appearances. In my opinion, this is a healthy attitude towards money. And something that gratifies me a great deal is the fact that my children are not at all conceited where money is concerned: they have never believed that such privileges might exonerate them from anything. Strangely enough, this attitude is not very common. In fact, it is quite rare, though I have never really understood why.

Being used to having money, which is very unfair, probably helps not being conceited about it, and the fact that some of it is earned also helps to prevent considering wealth as something sacred. The difference between people who earn money and those who do not, even if they are rich, is very obvious. Even as a child, I was aware of belonging to a privileged family. I believe that if you work in a meaningful way and are successful in the world of finance, you will acquire material wealth. This is also what the Jews and Protestants believe in a quasi-moralistic way, while the Catholics, who always feel guilty where money is concerned, experience it as one of the two great sins of our time, the other, of course,

ON MONEY

being sex. But if a person's main goal consists primarily of wanting to earn money, it is a mistake, because that should not be anyone's prime motivation. I say this from experience: you can waste your life and your talent in the quest for riches.

The privileges that money brings also entail responsibilities. I have always believed it was a duty to donate money, which is closer to Jewish thought, where generosity is linked to a sense of justice, than it is to the Christian idea, where it is associated with charity. I have established – in no particular order – several areas that take priority. In my mind, there is a large section for museums, which is quite extensive because the list is rather long, from the Louvre to the Musée des Arts décoratifs, including the Guimet, the Cluny, the Metropolitan, the Morgan Library, the National Gallery in London... Another area is public health, whether it is the New York Hospital, the American Hospital in Paris or departments headed by certain professors of medicine... The third relates to Jewish charities, on both sides of the Atlantic... the fourth concerns Catholic charities (in New York in particular), a large Catholic Medical School and charities in Haiti... There are various other good causes: a Black town in deepest Mississippi where I finance the free clinic and the community center, as well as individuals, like a young girl from northern France whose parents wrote me a very polite, honest letter saying they didn't have the means to allow her to study music.

For many years, I have corresponded with a young girl from the Ivory Coast whose educational fees I contribute to but whom I have never met... Recently, a man wrote to me because he didn't have enough money for his wife's funeral. I contribute to the upkeep of Jewish cemeteries in eastern France and I donate money to charities that work to prevent cruelty to animals... And this is something I desire to support financially because I consider it a charity like the others. I try to make sure that I have the means to make donations and to purchase works of art. I expect absolutely nothing in return, not even gratitude, which is something I do not believe in. I do these things in and for themselves and because I can. To tell the truth, they give me pleasure.

The main advantage of money – and this should never be forgotten – is freedom. My mother taught me this very early on, but I have often forgotten it because too many commitments prevent me from being free. In this respect, I was held back for a long time by the professional concerns that have filled my life. Nevertheless, money is a means to freedom. To be able to travel in the most luxurious conditions, wherever you like, whenever you like and without any financial limitations, to stay in a very good hotel even though you own several houses – which itself is an almost absurd luxury – all these things contribute to one's freedom. So it would never occur to me to think money has not played a role in my life, does not exist, is despicable or does not count. On the contrary, earning money by working, as I have done, has been one of the great currents that has carried me through life. It has allowed me to flow down the river rather than fighting my way upstream, and to gaze at the landscape, rather than having to paddle, which is infinitely more pleasant. I have still had to take the oars rather often, but under very favorable circumstances.

The price you pay for this is even greater isolation. It may sound ridiculous, but luxury sets you apart. And that is actually the desired goal: silence, space, the absence of difficulties... all these things isolate you. I could try to live another way. All I would have to do is change and make the decision to travel in economy... Lord knows that I do not believe there is any virtue in being very wealthy, and people shouldn't attach too much importance to it. I have known individuals whom I consider saints who were very wealthy. Not many, but there have been some...

Whether you like it or not, one third of the population will be wildly impressed simply because you have money. They don't see the real you, just a stack of banknotes. It doesn't matter to me, but it is disturbing because I do not think these people are seeing properly. Another third of the population will hate you and be envious of you at the same time because they think that you can do no good since you are essentially tainted. They believe you can't understand anything because you are rich. So only one third of the population reacts to you more or less normally. I think this is enormously limiting... but I have had no other experience. As a result, contact with other people is greatly reduced. From this perspective, men and women are in a more or less equal position. One third of women do not wish to speak to me either. They tell themselves: "He's going to think I'm motivated by self-interest."

This attitude backfires in a rather complicated way: because they are so impressed, they feel a need to avoid you. I believe more in this idea, however, than in the idea that women are self-seeking. I'm not saying that they do not exist, but, strangely enough, I haven't met many women like that... Perhaps I am just unbelievably naive but I really don't think I have. Then there are the men and women, especially in France, who, because of their philosophy, are very critical of a society that allows such inequalities. This causes problems, although not for me personally. However, you cannot avoid the fact that it is a problem for others. Children can sense this very well. They hate being taken to school in a car that is too expensive and make you drop them off at a discreet distance from the building. Among young people, making new friends can be more difficult. People talk to them about their father and, for whatever bit of celebrity he might have, if he is also very wealthy, that only adds to the problem.

What sets me apart most from French public opinion is their hateful or envious approach to money, as well as their attitude towards the past and the future. I really do not understand why today's world should be more frightening than yesterday's. Not that I do not understand why people are afraid of the modern world, I just don't see why they would not have been afraid of yesterday's world, which does not seem so wonderful to me... I witnessed how difficult life was for French rural farmers before the war and even during the Occupation. I do not see what their physical misery brought them in terms of moral grandeur. Once again, I cannot grasp the relationship between poverty and virtue, or between wealth and vice.

I remember that after the war, I was lucky enough – and I do consider it luck – to spend many afternoons in Harlem, at Friendship House, a charitable institution under the directorship of a black man who came from Oxford.

ON MONEY

Young people like myself would go there and volunteer to take packages, usually food before the weekend, to people who were so desperately poor that they had nothing to eat. After waiting around in the office, we would stroll through Harlem to deliver the packages. It was before the war in Algeria, when French people were extremely respected in black neighbourhoods, so it was a passport that opened every door. I never had any run-ins or encountered the slightest problem; on the contrary, I met very open, warm people. Poverty in America is nothing like what you would expect. They were so poor that they had nothing to eat, yet they had all sorts of electrical appliances: a refrigerator (with nothing in it), or a car (with no gas). Having seen this type of need first-hand made me understand how illusory material possessions can be when determining the true condition of people.

The fact that today's world is changing so very quickly can be disturbing in a certain way, but it also opens up many hidden possibilities. I do not dread the present, nor do I long for the past, and my travels have led me to believe that there are many virtues in current trends whose goal it is to create a more decent existence. No matter what you do or say, life in the past was horrendous almost everywhere, but it was hidden. Today, I wouldn't go so far as to say that the fact that life is more comfortable for many people changes the human condition. Happiness is an illusion that can last for rather a long time, perhaps even a lifetime. You are in love, you are going to have a baby, you get a better job, you go on vacation... There is always the hope that something exists that you can attain, but which remains elusive...

A TASTE FOR HAPPINESS

I am indifferent to the fascination that money arouses. I see myself as a man who is considerate, who lives very well and who loves his friends. But I am certainly not, in any way whatsoever, the mythical person that newspapers sometime spread rumors about, for better or for worse. I not recognize myself in these descriptions, and, moreover, there is so little resemblance to who I am that it doesn't even affect me. It is foreign to me... It seems almost a joke to talk about it... And yet, I am not modest, I believe I am intelligent, more so than many people... but I do not think I am important simply because I have money. And though we live in a world in which appearances mean a great deal, and where money – whether real or imagined – counts enormously, this is just one more illusion. Nevertheless, it can be socially harmful not to consider yourself important because other people end up agreeing with you.

Other people will have the opinion of you that you have of yourself, and for a very simple reason: they have no imagination and, consequently, they listen to you in order to form their own ideas. We have all known women who were not very physically attractive but who claimed that they were, so they were thought of as beautiful because everyone believed them. People look no deeper and that is fine. Imagine the number of individuals that people have to meet and assess, the number of judgments they have to make simply to cope in life. They're not going to waste yet more time coming to their own conclusions: they just repeat whatever you say about yourself. This is why you should never disparage yourself too much! Because whatever you say – for example, "I am incredibly talented at drawing" or "I am an amazing lover" – people will believe you. They will think it is true. So if you say: "I'm an idiot", they will believe that too. You have to be very careful about what you say!

Nevertheless, I have not succeeded in trying to appear important. Perhaps this is a kind of snobbery on my part. I think that people will either accept you or reject you; it's up to them, so it isn't really necessary to portray yourself as particularly colorful and pleasant to them. They will either accept you or they won't. Of course, you do have to try to be as charming as possible with other people, simply and principally so that you do not become bored. One of my daughters is very funny and I said to her one day, "You are very entertaining to talk to", to which she replied: "That's because I don't want to get bored!" That seemed completely fair to me because it is rare to become totally bored with a person with whom you can be amusing.

I cannot bear that the people I love should be dependent on me, so I do everything I can to make them independent, at least materially. If people attach so much value to money, it is because they are afraid of renouncing it because they are afraid they won't exist. It is true that the more you renounce money, the less important you are. If I have gotten along very well with priests all throughout my life, it is because I have been lucky enough – and this isn't true of everyone – to meet clergymen who had almost completely renounced money. They did not desire to exist in themselves, they existed in their faith, in their charity and even in carrying out their vocation, but they had clearly renounced money. Obviously, it is easier to do this for a great cause than for its own sake, otherwise you end up destroying yourself. People refuse to renounce money because they are afraid of what might happen: will I create a situation in which people walk all over me? Will no one give a damn about me? Will I even be able to tell what I want or desire? So they cling on to their arguments over money in order to exist. I fear that this might be the main cause of the fact that, in human societies, no matter what profession you carry out, you encounter the petty squabbles that make life much less pleasant than it could be. I have toyed with the idea, not much but a bit nonetheless, of what I call the monastic temptation, thinking that, deep down, I might actually be a very happy monk... However, I think there are certain vows that I would not like... Not the vows of poverty or obedience... To adhere to strict rules in order to become free but detached from worldly possessions, would probably suit me.

You can be free, but no longer entirely an individual. And I have always found that a superb idea!

I have always somewhat longed for total anonymity, which is one of the reasons why I like the United States: you can go unnoticed because outward signs of social distinction do not exist. If you are wealthy, you are someone successful, or lucky. As a general rule, everyone admires that. Wealth is not a true social value because it does not fundamentally change you in the eyes of other people. You may have more money but you are still the same person. Take someone who drives his Cadillac to the gas station and the attendant who pumps gas: there is no real class distinction. Being famous might be enjoyable, but that doesn't make any real difference either. Andy Warhol put it very well: "Everyone will have his fifteen minutes of fame". But we all know very well that it means nothing. I am exaggerating a little because Americans are impressed by fame, by actors in particular, but not exclusively. It may not be a question of a difference in social class, but it is a difference all the same. I once came out of my office and saw someone whose name had been in all the newspapers two weeks earlier because he'd been involved in a scandal and gone bankrupt. But people were going up to shake his hand, with no animosity, because he was famous. One of my former African American partners, whom I like very much, was an important lawyer and a friend of President Clinton when he became a banker at Lazard. Whenever we walked along together, it was rather touching to see a large part of the African American population coming up to say hello to him.

They didn't know him, but they said things like: "You once met my uncle..." It was obvious that he had no recollection of it at all, but he pretended to. He was a celebrity, a role model. But no one thought: "He's become a great man so I can't talk to him any more." That is one of the eminently likeable sides of the United States.

If I said that I could do without almost everything I have, no one would believe me. Money is one of life's pleasures and it is rather annoying to have less of it, but not all that annoying. I say this at the risk of sounding provocative. But we still shouldn't be reduced to being defined by what we own: that is certainly not the answer!

About the Author

A man of two countries, Michel David-Weill was born in France. He loves his native country and the United States, where he has spent more than half his life.

As senior partner at Lazard, an international investment firm, he led the firm for twenty-five years and was responsible for reuniting the London, Paris, and New York offices.

Passionate about the arts, David-Weill is a collector and a trustee of the New York Metropolitan Museum of Art and of the French National Museums.

A Taste for Happiness describes what he has learned about life during his long career.

Printed in Great Britain
by Amazon